For:

Lindsay, my beautiful wife.

When we are together life expands.

And for:

Adara, my daughter.

'You are an incredible girl'

HEAR HIS CALL

Meeting God Amidst Creation

Jon Plunkett

vine arts
publications

Song Lyrics used with permission – 'A Thousand Years' by Andy
Dorrat © 2005 Andy Dorrat. 'Hallelujah (your love is amazing)'
by Doerkson & Brown ©2000 Vineyard songs (UK/Eire). When
'I survey the Wondrous Cross' by Isaac Watts, Public Domain.
'Here is our King' & 'Come and Listen' by David Crowder
©2005 worshiptogether.com Songs / sixsteps Music / Adm. by
Kingswaysongs.com for the UK & Europe tym@kingsway.co.uk.
'The Kingdom Song' by Darrel Evans ©1997 Integrity's Hosanna!
Music / Sovereign Music UK reproduced with permission
sovereignmusic@aol.com

Quotations reprinted with permission of HarperCollins Publishers
Ltd
'The Lord of the Rings' ©J.R.R. Tolkien 1954

All other Quotations, Testimonies and Prose fully credited where
they appear.

Published by Vine Arts Publications
www. thevinechurch.com

131 Garvock Hill, Dunfermline, Fife, KY11 4JU

British Library Cataloguing in Publication Data: A catalogue entry
for this book can be obtained from the British Library.

ISBN: 0-9552881-0-X

Typeset by: Vine Arts Publications

Illustrations and cover design by Lindsay Plunkett

Printed and bound by CopyTECH UK Ltd. - Peterborough

Acknowledgements

Thanks to all who have walked with me in wild places, every experience has gone into shaping this book. To Simon Neil, Andrew Kerr and Ross Kerr: you three who have walked with me in the wildest places. I pray that none of you will ever touch the void. To David (Hammy) Hamilton and Jonathan (Jonny) Barclay for walking with me over the peaks and ridges of this adventurous Christian life. To Calum Mitchell for sharing a dream. To the Pastors and Elders of The Vine church for supporting a dream. To 'the seven', who became eight... soon to be nine – my Scottish family. To Petra Wilson for 'holding the fort' when there was work to be done. To Lenny Turk for your spiritual wisdom and the numerous cups of tea and chats in forests and on hillsides. To Mum and Dad of course, for support beyond the call of duty - Mum for encouraging me to try and for catching every fall. Dad, for those formative years when you would carry me on your back to the wild places you love. Thanks to Karen Dorrat for all the practical help, your proofreading skills and publishing knowledge.

And finally thanks to Lindsay for being the most incredible editor, critic, designer, supporter, adventurer, lover, wife and friend throughout every step of this journey.

CONTENTS

Foreword

The little Scottish Island of Iona is one of the most wild and wonderful places I have ever visited. It was twenty-five years ago, in this serenely beautiful and remote place, that God met with me in an amazing way. On bended knee, upon the rocky floor of a cave, tears streamed down my face. It was a moment of intimacy with God that was to shape the course of my life.

I sat there in God's presence and, looking out to sea, I vividly imagined St. Columba arriving in 563 AD, with his band of twelve noble men. They had arrived on these wild shores with the daunting purpose of spreading the gospel among people who were as wild as the lands they inhabited. What a challenge they faced, with none of the roads or transport we know today. They had faced danger with almost every step and there was certainly no media or telephones or Internet to aid the spread of their message! As I knelt there, I was convicted with the fact that we have it so comparatively easy in our age of comfort and convenience.

Twenty-five years on and I now find myself in many ways doing the same thing as St. Columba. I am investing my life in twelve men and spreading the gospel throughout

Scotland and beyond. Every human being needs to know wonderful intimacy with their Heavenly Father and I now live to see as many as possible hear that message.

'Hear His Call' is a masterpiece that will reinforce in your life just how much God desires to meet with you in an intimate way. He is passionate about you and longs to meet with you alone, just as any loving parent desires to care for and be with their child. This book is a clarion call to a generation that has almost lost the ability to rest, to be still, to be quiet, and to be alone with God amidst the beauty of His wild creation.

This is not another theory book. This is a book written by a man who eats, sleeps and breathes passion for God and for meeting with Him in 'wild places'. 'Hear His Call' is informative, instructive and pulsating with testimonies and insights that will thrill your heart and positively transform your life. This book will take pride of place on my bookshelf, alongside my Bible, and will be read and reread many times.

This timely and prophetic book is a cry from God's heart to you. It is a call that will encourage and inspire you to draw aside, to climb the mountain, to get out into the wild places like those so loved by the Celtic saints. It is a call to get out there and savour the beauty of God reflected in what He has made. It is a call to get out into His creation and be transformed forever as He meets intimately with you.

I wholeheartedly believe in the message and principles of this book and recommend that you read it and apply its message to your life.

Pastor Jimmy Dowds
The Vine Church, Scotland

Preface

It is my hope that this book will encourage more people to get out and meet with God amidst His natural creation. To do so is a life-enhancing experience, yet it is one that is both overlooked and undervalued. Amidst natural landscapes, the eyes are drawn from one scene of natural beauty to another, while the mind is propelled toward the Creator. From the creation of mankind, and in these times as much as ever, God's desire is to meet intimately with His people. The message of this book is that there is no better place to meet with Him than in the midst of what He has made. The diversity of the natural settings God has made is limitless. Even the same scene can be changed from one day to the next, as autumn leaves are blown from the trees, or the snows of winter arrive, or spring flowers rise rapidly from the earth, or the vibrant green of summer leaves glow with life. This intimate detail and harmonious diversity is inspirational, it fuels intrigue, wonder and awe, for all of it reveals something of the Creator and provides us with powerful evidence of His ongoing and immeasurable love.

Yet this is not a book written simply to encourage more

Christians to enjoy this spiritual experience in some selfish way. When Jesus spent time alone in wild places He came back and changed the world, and so should we. He tells us to go out and make disciples, to change the world of those who do not yet know Him. We can go out to wild places, meet with God, and return so radically changed that like Jesus we can impact the lives of those we meet. Furthermore, these wild places offer us a site free from everyday distractions, where the scenery raises questions of our existence and purpose in life. The whole of the natural world can stir questions deep within. Questions that can remain buried or glossed over by a life lived in a world of impermanence. Who am I? Why am I here? Where am I going? There is something about being surrounded by wild landscapes that causes us to ask these questions, and to seek the answers.

There are many accounts of biblical heroes and more recent godly leaders who have positively changed the course of history through meeting with God amidst His wild creation. These men and women have set aside time to be in wild places alone with their heavenly Father, and as a result have had a lasting impact upon the world. Imagine a body of people whose daily priority is to spend time with their Creator and Father, to worship and develop a heart relationship with Him. Imagine a church of people who are fully dependent upon Him, people who have incredible clarity in their independent and collective spiritual vision, and each with a drive for the ministry to which they have been called. This would, like the early church, be a force to be reckoned with, a group of people that impacts the culture around it and that changes the world.

The experience of meeting with God is hard to capture in writing, for it goes far deeper than words can convey. Yet among these pages I hope that you will find a glimmering of the depth of experience that can be gained through meeting with God, particularly amidst His wild creation. I hope that God will use these words to impact your life. I hope that some inspiration will be found to make these times with God a regular part of your relationship with Him. I know that if you do, you will find it a life-changing experience. I have sat, stood, walked and climbed in many wild places and have dreamed of playing a part in inspiring more people to meet intimately with the living God. I dream of a world where prayers of praise rise from forests, loch-sides, coastlines, and moorlands. Up from hillsides, marshes, valleys and mountaintops. Even up from tundra, jungle, plains and prairies. I dream that these places would be sites where we get to know God intimately and where people who don't yet know Him, will give their lives completely to Him. I pray that in some small way, this book will help make this wild dream become a reality.

SETTING THE SCENE

A Call for All

'Since the creation of the world God's invisible
qualities - his eternal power and divine nature - have
been clearly seen, being understood from what has
been made so that men are without excuse'
(Romans 1:20).

Steady upward progress leaves a sleepy world sinking into the darkness below. The surrounding environment is changing...has changed...will change more as I ascend through the early hours of a dark winter pre-dawn. The warm protecting bubble of the car has, with the slam of a door, the turn of a key and a number of excited steps, become a rough track through scratchy Spruce trees. My inner heater is kicking in as these Spruces turn to scattered Pines and Birch. Even in the torchlight the bark of the Birch appears white and somehow more reassuring than the dark caverns lurking among the Spruce branches. The track disappears and reappears under patchy snow as the last trees fall away below. Then the path is gone for good under a continuous blanket of crisp white snow. The torch is no longer needed, as all around the snow-covered hanging corrie* is floodlit with the luminescent glow of the moon.

* A 'bite' out of the side of a hill, often containing a loch, where the ground rises on three sides of the flat area and drops away on the other.

Step after step over trackless snow brings me to the Belach* where another dimension joins the view as the ground now drops away to the North on one side, the South on the other. To the West I turn and onto the long summit ridge where my every sense tingles in response to this eerily-beautiful environment. I watch as every breath floats off into the cold air. I feel the prickle of condensed and frozen breath on my hood and beard. I hear every step as the frozen, icy crust breaks and my foot sinks into the softer snow beneath. I taste the fresh, pure air, and feel its chill deep in my throat. My eyes drink in the frozen patterns in the snow and the contrast of the protruding black rock. I stare amazed at the ice crystals on the higher rocks, reflecting a light that has changed now from star-strewn blackness with its lunar floodlight to a deep navy where only the brighter stars are visible. The light is becoming the half-light of dawn, so revered by the Celtic peoples. The summit still looks distant but this light plays tricks, for in it things look bigger and steeper and further away than they actually are. Suddenly I find the ground dropping off in all directions. I can't go any higher and so it is on the cold high summit I stand.

To the North I see a glimmer of light - just a faint glow. As I watch I notice more becoming visible, for what I see are the first rays of sunlight catching the highest points of this fine land of the Scots. The frozen, lonely summits of the hills start to glow. A few, then a few more, then hundreds of them, changing from dim reds and pinks to brightest fiery orange. Behind to the Southeast the sun is edging surprisingly quickly over the horizon.

I realise that I too am standing on one of those fiery islands of light, separated from civilisation by a sea of thick darkness. For this day I am one of the only people, perhaps the only one to look on, awe-struck, as the first rays of a new day strike land. I drop to my knees, partly through an overwhelming confusion about how to respond to such a scene but mostly because of something much deeper than the physical. The physical has triggered the spiritual. I

* Also known as gap, coll or pass, this is the area where two hills join and the ground drops on two sides and rises on the other two.

could cry or perhaps cry out. I could fall face down in the snow or jump up and down, but I don't. I just kneel there, watching and feeling. Feeling elated. Feeling privileged. Feeling small. Feeling intoxicated by this mix, and above all feeling an intense awe of the Creators creation, and of the Creator Himself, with whom I am more certain than ever before I have a genuine and close relationship. I have gazed at this scene and learned about Him. I have learned of His incredible attention to detail, His immense power and ongoing control of this place called earth. Through His creation I have come to know more, much more, of Him. I feel as though in this moment I have come to know more of Him than in the rest of my life prior to this point and place.

On that incredible winter morning it was as though God used the snow-covered landscape as a vast stage. Sun and moon were the spotlights as the story was played out in the grandest of theatres. The story was one of drawing closer to God than I had ever thought possible.

In my life I have had many significant encounters with God but it is amidst His wild creation many of my deepest and most transforming encounters have occurred. More often than not these experiences have been well below the summit heights: by the side of a stream, at the coast, in a forest, or on the valley floor. Almost every time I have set foot in the wilds I have come back with a deeper relationship with God, and increased heart knowledge of His call on my life. I believe that the call to meet God in His wild creation is a call for everyone... a call for all. It is this conviction that has compelled me to write this book in an attempt to encourage more Christians to enter the wild areas of our lands and there draw closer than ever to our Father.

So why is it that more Christians do not leave society, even for a short time, and get out into natural creation to meet God? Why is it that to contemplate creation has become nice to sing about rather than an incredible thing to do? Why do we claim to love God our Father, the Creator of all and yet believe it is justified to spend so little or no time appreciating the world He has made? Why do we believe that the desire to place ourselves in untainted places and learn more of our Creator is something that is only suitable for a certain type of person? Is God's natural creation, and time spent in it, really something that should be of importance to those who know Him?

Jesus often withdrew to wild places for rest, prayer and divine meetings. He set the example.

'After he had dismissed them, he went up a mountainside by himself to pray.' (Matthew 14:23)

'Very early in the morning, while it was still dark, Jesus got up, left the house and went off to a solitary place where he prayed.' (Mark 1:35)

'Jesus went up on a mountainside and called to him those he wanted, and they came to him.' (Mark 3:13)

'One of those days Jesus went out to a mountainside to pray, and spent the night praying to God.' (Luke 6:12)

'Each day Jesus was teaching at the temple, and each evening he went out to spend the night on the hill called the Mount of Olives.' (Luke 21:33)

'Jesus, knowing that they intended to come and make him king by force, withdrew again to a mountain by himself.' (John 6:15)

'Then Jesus went up on a mountainside and sat down with his disciples.' (John 6:3)

'Jesus went as usual to the Mount of Olives.' (Luke 22:39)

'After six days Jesus took with him Peter, James and John the brother of James and led them up a high mountain by themselves' (Matthew 17:1)

'Then the eleven disciples went to Galilee, to the mountain where Jesus had told them to go.' (Matthew 28:16)

'We ourselves heard this voice when we were with him on the sacred mountain.' (2 Peter 1:18)

These are just a selection of the numerous scriptures that record Jesus spending time in wild creation. Many of the accounts state 'as usual' or 'again' Jesus went out alone to the wild. This implies that there will have been many other times in wild areas that Jesus met with His Father.

Jesus used wild sites in a variety of ways. We see Him using them as a place of retreat, to evade those making demands of Him. We see Jesus using these locations as a place to meet with the disciples, a place for solitary prayer, as a site for miracles, a place for preaching and teaching large groups, and for the healing of many. Jesus used these natural sites as places to be free from busyness and distraction. And we see, on numerous occasions, Jesus explicitly requesting that the disciples take themselves out of the towns and onto mountainsides, hillsides and seashores. Often we read that He led them out into such places. This was obviously very important to Jesus, so when we ask ourselves 'what would Jesus do if He were on earth today?' then we can be quite certain that He would set aside time in a quiet place amidst wild creation to pray and spend time with His Father. Through such times Jesus knew what He was here on earth to do. Through times of prayer, of direct contact with His father, He knew that He must die and rise again. As a result of this we can have eternal life.

Throughout the scriptures God uses wild creation in three main ways. Firstly, God meets directly with people in places where they are surrounded by His natural creation. Often they will have been called or drawn to the site by God. Secondly, the creation itself reveals aspects or qualities of the Creator and leads to a better understanding of Him. And thirdly, God uses His creation in miraculous ways to benefit or speak to His people. More often than not these can be seen as times when God changes the natural order, ability or structure of creation. Although these can be seen as distinct categories of God's use of wilderness, there are overlaps and similarities between them. There are many examples of each.

In terms of being used as a meeting place for direct

encounter with God, one of the first biblical examples is Hagar with her son Ishmael, driven from the camp of Abraham, meeting with God in the desert of Beersheba (Genesis 21:17-18). Alone in the desert and desperate, is the setting where God meets, comforts and provides for Hagar and her son. Later we read of how God led Abraham and his young son Isaac high onto the slopes of Mount Moriah (Genesis 22:2-19). Moses also spoke with God through the burning bush on the side of Mount Sinai (Exodus 3:1-6). We read that, years later, Elijah sought refuge on the slopes of Mount Sinai and there God spoke to Him through a whisper on the breeze (1 Kings 19:8-12). The Disciples, led by Jesus up the slopes of Mount Hermon, witnessed Him meeting supernaturally with Moses and Elijah, and then heard God speak in an audible voice (Matthew 17:1, Mark 9:2, Luke 9:28). There are countless other examples of God calling people out into His wild creation and there meeting directly with them.

The second powerful way that God uses creation is to reveal aspects of His character. Many examples can be seen in the Psalms, where contemplation of creation has enabled a fuller understanding of the Creator and an increased intimacy with Him. In Psalm 93 the Psalmist gains understanding of God's power through contemplation of the seas:

> "Mightier than the thunder of the great waters, mightier than the breakers of the sea - the Lord on high is mighty."
>
> (Psalm 93:4)

The Psalmist gazes at the seas and knows more of the strength of God. Similarly the skies are seen to reveal aspects of their creator:

> "The heavens declare the glory of God; the skies proclaim the works of His hands. Day after day they pour forth speech; night after night they display knowledge."
>
> (Psalm 19:1&2)

And again in Psalm 36:

> "Your love, O Lord, reaches to the heavens, your
> faithfulness to the skies. Your righteousness is like
> the mighty mountains, your justice like the great
> deep."
>
> (Psalm 36:5&6)

The Psalmist has learned more about certain aspects of God's character through time spent amidst His creation. Elsewhere in the Bible, the entire nation of Israel saw God's power as Moses met with God on Sinai and the whole mountain was enveloped in smoke and trembled (Exodus 19:16-26). Through looking at God's natural creation, these people, and many others, knew more of the Creator.

Lastly, there are many references in scripture where God uses the natural world to aid His people miraculously. God parts the water and creates a route for Israel through the sea so they can escape the pursuing Egyptians (Exodus 14:21&22). God provides manna with the dew and Quail to land in the Israelite camp in the desert of Sin (Exodus 16:13-18). God causes a donkey to speak to Balaam (Numbers 22:21-24). God causes midday to become dark (Matthew 27:45, Mark 15:33, Luke 23:44&45). God calms a storm (Matthew 8:26, Mark 4: 39, Luke 8:24).

Time and time again God used natural creation to benefit the lives of His people and their relationship with Him. These divine encounters were not reserved for a certain type of person. From servant girls, to masters, shepherds to Kings, individuals to entire nations, we see natural creation playing an important role. In all cases the result is an increased knowledge of Yahweh, The Creator God.

When I have heard music I like, I am often drawn to find out more about the singer, songwriter or composer. Or when I have read a snippet of writing in a review, or a quote in a book, I have often bought the book referred to. I am not content with the small sample of something that seems so worth having. My desire is to have it in full, and through this desire I come to know not only the work, but much of its creator as well. What about when God's love is revealed to us and we finally acknowledge Him as our Saviour? Could it be so many of us continue to struggle because we settle for the snippets? Could it be so many drift away from God because the reviews from the Sunday pulpit are as far as their knowledge of the Saviour goes?

True love inspires a complete interest in the loved one. My wife, Lindsay, works as a professional artist and I do not just want to know her through conversation or through others' comments. I want to know all of her. I want to know what her interests are and why she finds them interesting. I want to know what pleases her and I want to know what does not. I want to understand her creativeness, and so I spend time looking at her artistic creations for in them are revealed aspects of Lindsay herself. Admittedly I am drawn to her work anyway as her paintings and other art works capture deep aspects of God's immensity, His peace and the beauty of His creation in ways that go far beyond the limitations of spoken or written word. By engaging with her creation I get to know her in more depth: depth that words fail to capture. Similarly, through time spent meeting with God amidst His natural creation, I get a more in-depth heart knowledge of God the creator, God my Father. I do not feel that I can love God with all my heart, all my soul and all my mind if I do not take the time and make the effort to leave man's world of society and enter God's creation. I need to get out and enjoy the beauty, for when I see beauty in some wild place, I see powerful and compelling aspects of the God who loves me and has my life in His hands. Beauty drew me to Lindsay and beauty draws me to God. In God's creation there is beauty, and it draws me out into such places and there I learn. Many see this beauty, and as a result God's wild creation has been the subject of or inspiration for countless great masterpieces: stunning works of art created in response to the surrounding creation. Above all the natural creation is beautiful because in it we learn of and experience something of the invisible qualities of God, His eternal power and Divine Nature. It is a beautiful place that is now missed by many.

Concrete and tarmac, central-heating and air-conditioning, twenty-four hour noise and entertainment through television and radio, global interconnection through internet and telecommunications - these things have, for many, taken the place of the carpets of grass and heather, the suns rays and fresh breezes, contemplation and silence, stillness and peace. Now we walk through a world where the whole natural landscape can be disconnected from our experience. Whole lives can be lived in an environment that is separated almost entirely from natural creation. The very creation our Father created and was pleased with. If we walk into the wild creation now, we are among the few who do. Many people will pass through it of course, but this passing through so often occurs in heated or air-conditioned cars with the music blaring as they hum along smooth roads disconnected from the world outside the windows. The connection with the earth has gone. So the structure of society itself has come between many of us and our creator God. We are separated from the beauty of wild creation. We are separated from the power and love of God that is displayed in these places. We need to actively seek God and set aside time to meet with Him in such settings.

God is calling us to draw close to Him. His desire is for us to set aside time just to be with Him. Natural creation is an ideal place to learn more of God. Contemplating what He has made is vital for developing a deeper and healthier relationship with Him. To say that it is too cold, too wet, too physical or too time-consuming is like saying that fasting causes too much hunger, prayer is too distracting and evangelism is too embarrassing! They are not justifiable excuses, but are an all-too-typical human reaction to divine calling. We need to learn more of Him. We need to know intimacy with Him. Our spiritual health is dependent upon it. God's natural creation is a site suited to developing a fuller heart knowledge of Him.

This time with God is never time wasted. Time alone with no distractions is time that God will use to still our hearts and clarify our vision. This time away is vital. It is vital to our relationship with our Father, and vital to remaining effective in the areas of ministry and servanthood He has called us into. Just look at Jesus and His regular withdrawal to wild places for rest and prayer. Even when death was imminent we find Jesus alone on the Mount of Olives. Jesus knew how important time alone with His Father would be for the coming hours. There are many more examples. In fact almost all major biblical ministries involved time set-aside specifically in the wilderness to seek God. I wonder would the Psalms of David be so intimate if David had not spent time alone with God surrounded by the rocky landscape? Would Moses have heard the call so clearly and embraced it so fully if he had not spent time alone on hills and in valleys? Would he have heard the call at all if he had not ventured out into these places? Would the Israelites, led into battle by Joshua, have had victory if Moses had placed himself with his men on the front line, rather than on the heights with his staff held high and his focus upon God? Would John the Baptist have effectively prepared the way if he had lived his life like everyone else in the bustle of society, rather than alone in the desert? God could have revealed Himself and His call on these biblical heros lives in another setting. Nothing is beyond the power of God. However, He chose not to. He chose to reveal himself amidst and through His own creation. He revealed His call on these wild lives in wild untamed places. Through listening to God and following His direction they realised they were playing a part in a much bigger story. If only we could more regularly grasp hold of the infinitely bigger picture, then how much more effective, dynamic, and exciting our lives could be!

Although times have changed and few of us now shepherd goats on hillsides, or mend nets by the shores, lead armies through deserts or travel on remote country paths, our lack of time spent in God's natural creation cannot be justified. It means only that we live in an era where more effort is required to spend time in such places. Seeking God is something we must specifically set out to do, rather than something naturally experienced in the course of our day. We need to spend time in His presence. What better place to do this than amidst the natural world He created! Get out of the office during the lunch break. Head for the nearest park or most natural place you can find. Instead of having a coffee with breakfast, take a flask, leave early, and spend some time at a spot in the country. Or simply get off the bus or train at an earlier stop, or park your car further from your workplace and spend some time appreciating the vastness of the sky while you pray!

> "The heavens declare the glory of God; the skies proclaim the works of his hands. Day after day they pour forth speech; night after night they display knowledge. There is no speech or language where their voice is not heard. Their voice goes out into all the earth, their words to the ends of the world."
> (Psalm 19:1-4)

Creation and the truth it reveals crosses all cultures and languages. National differences and shifting trends and fashions are transcended by the omniscience and omnipotence of God revealed through creation. Natural places, supernaturally created by an unchanging God. Our God 'the Rock of Ages', the Alpha and Omega, the Beginning and the End, is not affected by fashions and trends. Through this physical and mental separation from culture, and the intimate experience of God amongst and through His creation, we as individuals, and collectively as the church, can remain relevant and vibrant in any age or culture.

This is definitely a call for every Christian. Everyone can access wild places and there meet with God. I think many people would be surprised at the accessibility of even the more remote areas. Simply because the heated, comfortable car with all its onboard entertainment cannot get us there does not make a place inaccessible. Yes it may at times be less convenient and comfortable to walk to some of these places and to meet with God there rather than in a familiar indoor setting, but in many ways it will be infinitely more rewarding.

In my work I have the pleasure of getting paid to lead people with learning disabilities out into these natural sites to which I refer. Through this 'work' I have come to know beyond doubt that it is not physical impairment or difficulty in walking that prevents access to such wild places, but lack of will or motivation. Learning disabilities all too often are accompanied by physical problems and conditions. I have watched, with bated breath, as individuals have precariously crossed a level floor from one side of a room to another. Getting many of these individuals on and off buses that are not specially adapted has proven a good test for teamwork and man-handling skills. Yet I have seen these same individuals travel over rough ground in order to reach remoter wild areas, even over hilltops on wild camping trips. These individuals, who when crossing a room, seem to push the laws of balance, have seen more remote areas than many 'able-bodied' individuals. No, it is not the physical condition, but lack of willpower that determines who is able and who is not. These 'disabled' individuals have scaled the rocky heights of Scotland's highest mountain, they have crossed wide rivers with fast flowing water drenching their legs, and spent nights in bothies* and in the wildest of campsites. These individuals have seen incredible sights, listened to the melody of natural sounds, tasted air that is so much fresher, smelled the earth and heather and felt the pulse of wild creation as it points to its Creator.

And again we look to Jesus, whom we should emulate. Did Jesus meet in places that were convenient? No. For example in Matthew 15:29 we read- "Then He (Jesus) went up on a mountainside and sat down." It is interesting to note who then came to Him in this wild spot as Matthew 15:30 tells us "Great crowds came to Him, bringing the lame, the blind, the crippled, the mute and many others." Their lack of physical ability did not prevent their coming. They had the desire and the will to get there and so, with some help, they did reach the spot. Also in this chapter we can note that again Jesus was alone in a wild place, but then that same wild place became the chosen site for a miraculous meeting with a crowd larger than many churches dream of. In that

* Bothies are basic shelters scattered throughout the Scottish Highlands, often consisting of little more that a roof and four walls.

place many were healed. The mute spoke, the crippled were made well, the lame walked and the blind received their sight. We read that the people then praised God who had healed them. I wonder how many praised with their eyes wide open, particularly among those healed of blindness, gazing out in awe over the grandeur, knowing that the same God who created everything they could now see, had just enabled them to see it. How they must have praised! I wonder did they recognise the scale, the vastness of His power, and yet realise that He loved each and every one of them as an individual within this whole?

I have also been in places with groups of children who are almost as wild as the environment itself. These children, defined as 'Children at Risk', are the ones whom classrooms cannot contain, and for whom the rules of society are there simply to be broken. Hyperactivity, Attention Deficit Disorder, unruliness, learning disabled, each of them carry a label. For them to listen for even five minutes is hailed as progress. I have watched these wild restless children listening, enthralled, to a countryside ranger, as he points out the various life forms in a slow-moving burn*. I have watched them sit still among the heather as he tells them how the geology surrounding them was formed. I have watched the 'group bully' become the group leader. A leader who spends himself in helping his peers cross rivers, and to get their tents up. I have watched the child with the learning disability discover some new natural wonder. I have seen the joy on his face as he reveals it to his friends, as he the 'unteachable' becomes the teacher. I have watched as the child with the attention deficit remains at the burnside long after the others have moved onto something else. The ranger has left, the others are in their tents, the leaders are preparing dinner, and there he stands, poking and prodding the banks and bed of the burn, lost in a world of exploration and discovery, fully focused on what he is doing. These children crave reality. They crave real adventure in a world that is solid and full of meaning. These children are just like all of us. We all need to get out and explore what

* A 'burn' is a small stream.

our heavenly Father has made.

This is not a call to become a hill walker, rambler or hiker. This is not escapism. This is not a selfish pursuit or a distraction from the more important things in life. Neither is it connected to ability, gender, age, cultural position or status. This is a call to meet with God in places where the sights, sounds, smells, tastes and textures have been created by Him and continue to declare His glory and proclaim the works of His hands. Places that continue to reveal His invisible qualities so that we can know Him more intimately. It is something for everyone. We all need time set apart specifically for meeting with God. And there are no better places than those set amidst His natural creation. This awesome Creator desires that we call Him Father. Jesus has set an example for us to follow. If we live like Him then we will find ourselves heading out to find some quiet spot to spend time with our Father. In doing so we step fully into the adventure of a life with God at the fore. This call is a call for all, a call to step into the natural creation that our Father has surrounded us with and there meet with Him.

How Wild a Wilderness?

Way up in the far North, upon the high summit of Ben Hope we stand together. *The view in every direction is incredible from this most northerly of Scotland's Munros. From here Lindsay and I feel as though we can see the whole northern section of this beautiful land, as though staring down on the most vivid of maps. The curving horizon forms its topmost edge. We are small again, lost in the vastness of this wild world. We stand together, silent, in awe and wonder and respect of God's immense creation and through it we know Him more.*

I am alone and feel it. The wind grows fiercer and the rain falls heavier. I press myself harder against this huge shelter stone and given its angle I should be dry. But this is Scotland where wind-blown rain comes horizontally! I know where I am but looking out into the greyness I feel that I could be anywhere. Well, anywhere cold, wet and thickly misty. It swirls all around me, like breath on a freezing day, shrouding the land in mystery. I can see but a few feet from my shelter. I feel excited somehow. It is almost as though I can hear the solitude. My inner senses are impacted too. This swirling damp distorts my concepts of time and space, even logic and reason. Things seem simultaneously closer and further away than they actually are. I think I see things, then they disappear... just drifting shapes in the mist. There is little room for fear though, just intrigue. Intrigue for the mystery of God revealed through this misty landscape and through it I know Him more.

Out through the door and down the lane to a destination only minutes away by foot. My daughter Adara sits in her comfy rucksack seat, cosy, gazing all around. She trusts me fully as I climb over the dry-stone wall, looking on as I push past the briers and brambles. She's too young for words but as she watches the swans through the rushes and reeds I know she loves these places. The low winter sun is setting and laying a golden path across the water, right to my feet. Adara's beautiful little face glows in the reflected light from the golden river. Every detail around feels like evidence of God's ongoing love for mankind, for me, for Adara and for His wild creation. I praise Him for the little creation on my back, and for this evidence of His love in His creation, and through it I know Him more.

Midnight, and Lindsay and I are just outside the cottage where we lived at the time, standing at the edge of a field. The stillness is striking. The wind that has blown the first brown leaves of autumn from the branches has dropped and now stopped. Where does it come from? Where does it go? Bright moonlight floods the fields and trees and the hills beyond those. Lindsay comments that it really does feel as though all creation knows He is coming and is poised in anticipation of that moment. We wonder if this is how it will be, if suddenly creation everywhere will signal His coming with its electric stillness, the deepest of calms before the greatest of storms, when the skies will be filled with glory. Despite the tingle of anticipation in this stillness there is immense peace. We stand still, silently enjoying the feelings and thoughts evoked by the scene, appreciating the stillness of His creation and through it we know Him more.

Wilderness... A spiritually difficult time or a place of natural wonder? A barren place where little can be gained from the land or a place of invaluable beauty? A place to be protected and conserved or a wild area not controlled by man? Chaotic and uninhabitable or a place for scientific study? A vast area of desert, the Polar caps, National Parks, great mountain ranges? Many different images come to mind when we hear the word wilderness. If your image of wilderness is predominantly negative then I hope to challenge that view, for God is calling His people to draw close to Him amidst His wild creation.

For Christians, the word 'wilderness' is probably most often used in relation to a spiritually-challenging time. This image might refer to a time of spiritual battle like Jesus in His forty days in the wild desert region of the Jordan valley, or a spiritually dry time like the Israelites' forty-year wilderness journey. This popular image of a spiritual wilderness can give a wrong impression of the geographical wild sites. It links the wild place with a negative time spiritually. These sites however, provided positive places for the overcoming of spiritual hardships. In the wilderness Jesus found the solitude he required to meet intimately with His Father so He could then resist the temptations of Satan. In this wild site He fasted and prayed and drew close to His Father. In the wild site He overcame the enemy and then walked back to civilization as the victor.

The Israelites found a place where they relied on God alone as He led them by way of a pillar of cloud during the day and a pillar of fire by night. He was also supernaturally providing food for them in the desert, where naturally none should have been found. Every morning the Israelites gathered manna that appeared miraculously with the dew. Through this reliance on God alone they became physically, emotionally and spiritually cut off from their dependence on the Egyptians. A whole generation died in the desert, and the new generation grew in a place that was free from the cultural influence of other nations. The wilderness provided a culturally-neutral site where the nation of Israel could develop as God intended. I wonder how many more years or centuries this would have taken had they remained within the relative safety of slavery to the Egyptians? I wonder would they have developed into the nation God desired them to be at all? Would they have experienced such freedom or seen as many miracles? In the desert wilderness they simultaneously experienced physical hardship and spiritual blessing. Through their time spent in the desert they developed a healthy, holy fear of the awesome power of their Creator. God became the centre of their culture and their lives. So while the wilderness was at times physically difficult, it was also entirely beneficial. The Israelites' spiritual wilderness was brought to an end through time spent in the physical wilderness. Their time in the desert prepared the nation of Israel for the Promised Land. So it is important to remember that while spiritual wilderness may be referred to negatively, the physical place can be the site where precious and much needed time with God is spent. It can be the place where He provides, and as a result, it is a place where victory is gained over the hardships.

When we enter the physical wilderness with a genuine desire to meet with God, and put Him first in our lives, blessing is the result. When in a spiritual wilderness with all its confusion and uncertainty, perhaps the order of the physical wilderness is the place to overcome it. In the busyness of a hectic pace of life, with little time for extended periods of prayer and bible study or praise and contemplation, many Christians struggle. A spiritual wilderness can be the result. But spend some time meeting with God amidst wild creation, and the order and peace found there, I am convinced, can start us on the journey out of our spiritual wilderness.

There is a wealth of peace to be found in meeting with our Father in natural places, yet most of the attention these places get in media circles is negative. When natural disasters strike, man usually looks for something or someone to blame. We have on the whole become too quick to allocate blame and negativity to wilderness and to natural phenomena such as floods, earthquakes, storms and so on. Many fatalities have occurred during these phenomena that have been labelled 'natural disasters' or 'Acts of God' and yet have actually been due to man's manipulation and abuse of the environment. High buildings, built cheaply and containing more homes and offices to make the builders and developers more money do not require much shaking before they fall over. Flat land by a riverside is a prime site for building because it is cheaper. Then, as the climate changes (partly due to pollutants, the waste products of mans' ways of life), we ask how God could allow such destructive flooding? God has created a whole natural world around us. Often it is through indirect abuse of these places that disasters then occur. Perhaps these things should be more commonly referred to as 'By-acts of Man'! Look beyond these popular images however, to God's creation without man's interference of it, and we find a place of beauty, order, and life. A place where we can meet with God and feel His peace flood into our lives.

This is a dark world I am passing through, under the thick canopy of dark green. I duck under and push through branches that have long been dead. Their needles have fallen and now coat the forest floor. High above, the healthy branches drink in the light so that little reaches through. Very little grows in this dank place. Despite the tops moving in the wind and the creak of gently-swaying trunks, the air down here is still and stifled. It feels as though I could speak and the words would stop just beyond my lips as they push against the heavy air. I could have gone around the perimeter of this Spruce plantation, but I thought the direct route straight through would be faster. Now I see my mistake as, in places, I am reduced to crawling on all fours as branches pull at my clothes. Brown needles jag my hands and knees, a sharp reminder that the direct route is not always the fastest. I am deep in these woods now, and reluctant to turn back. I push on, through the branches and the still, musty air. Despite the scratches, it is an intriguing environment. Birdsong rings out from the treetops and glimpses of blue sky beyond the canopy evoke a certain anticipation.

Up ahead a patch of bright light breaks up the dimness. I

push towards it, and draw closer to a green glowing island of vibrant light and life. In some past storm a number of trees have been uprooted or snapped near their base. It must have been a powerful wind to snap such thick wood as though it were no more than a thin brittle branch like those I have been struggling through. I sit at the edge of this welcoming pool of sunlight. It is no more than twenty metres across. The ground is uneven with large stumps and mounds of earth where trees have been pushed over, roots and all. Beside some of these root-plates are pools of water, filling the hole left as the roots pull upward taking earth and boulders with them. Trees, their branches bare and much of the bark gone, lie in a variety of shapes, angles and directions. The timber is softening, decaying. Yet I look around, and realise that I am not looking at a site of chaotic destruction. From the old trees I see numerous fungi and mosses. Ferns drink in the light that now reaches the forest floor. Grasses are replacing the needles. Wood Sorrel grows, with tiny white flowers that are framed beautifully against the glowing green. Insects and flies buzz lazily through the warm air, spot-lit by the sun. The air is fresher and I feel warmth. The birds, previously only heard, are now seen as they flit about the treetops. They swoop in and feed on the insects. The insects help break down the tough timbers they feed on. The soil is filled with nutrients from the decaying wood. New plants thrive in the sun-warmed and nutrient-rich soil.

This little island is the opposite of chaos. It is ordered. The wind, an external force, has created a chance for life. It cleared a way for the light to shine through. With that, a whole delicately-balanced system has been established. It is a system that has resulted in beauty, diversity, order and life.

I sit bathed in light and I think of our world and the similarities between it and this little island. I look at the surrounding sea of trees. I think of our world, surrounded by infinite space. I think of the force that caused these stems to snap and trees to uproot. I think how we have been created by the all-powerful God of the Universe. Our God, who said 'let there be light', and there was light. Our God, the Creator of all, who established our world and placed us upon it. Life was breathed into His creation. In a world that was perfect, mankind fell. The world plunged into the sea of darkness. But light pierced through and by grace and mercy unrivalled, we were given the greatest second chance of all. A way was made for life. I sit on my island and think that while God is the initial Creator, Jesus is like the powerful wind that makes a way for light and life eternal. The Holy Spirit is like the sun that warms the heart and brings intimacy to this living relationship.

Here I am, stumbling through dark thickets. Suddenly I have come upon a place where it all seems so obvious. So much order. So much delicate balance. So much perfection and harmony. I look around and as I do I grasp more fully the perfect plan God has for mankind and for me. I look around and know that I stand before the greatest Creator of all.

If something is not under man's control then we must ask whose control it is under. Gales and earthquakes, meteorites and floods, volcanic eruptions and avalanches all remind us of our fragility. They leave trails of damage, smash houses, cause road and bridge closures, shipping and flight delays, topple trucks and cars and generally wreak havoc with daily life. Yet, like the wind, these things have been in place long before the comfortable, technological, materialistic ways of man. Many people now have no belief in a God of the universe. Many have now swallowed a lie and believe they are simply living in the here and now, living a random life. Many have been blinded to the order and harmony and balance in God's wild creation. No wonder any wild force is viewed negatively for if it is not under man's control, and there is no God of love and goodness, then it is something to be feared.

For Christians, though, we have the joy of knowing that we live not only for the here and now, but for a much greater purpose. We know that we are saved by the love and grace of the Living God of the Universe. We know who is in control of all things. When God speaks to Job, He leaves no doubt that He is in control of His Creation:

'Where were you when I laid the earth's
foundation?
Have you ever given orders to the morning,
Or shown the dawn its place, that it might take the
earth by the edges and shake the wicked out of it?
Have you journeyed to the springs of the sea or
walked in the recesses of the deep?
Have you entered the storehouses of the snow or
seen the storehouses of hail, which I reserve for
times of trouble, for days of war and battle?
What way is it to the place where the lightning is
dispersed, or the place where the east winds are
scattered over the earth?
Can you bind the beautiful Pleiades?
Can you loose the cords of Orion?
Can you bring forth the constellations in their
seasons or lead out the bear with its cubs?
Can you raise your voice to the clouds and cover
yourself with a flood of water?
Do you send lightning bolts on their way?
Who provides food for the raven when its young
cry out to God and wander about for lack of food?
Do you know when the mountain goats give birth?
Do you watch when the doe bears her fawn?
Do you give the horse his strength or clothe his
neck with a flowing mane?
Does the hawk take flight by your wisdom and
spread his wings towards the south?
Does the eagle soar at your command and build his
nest on high?
Who has a claim against me that I must pay?
Everything under heaven belongs to me.
                    (Job 38,39&41:selected verses)

Amidst natural creation we can look around and meet
with our God who created and is in ultimate control of all we
see. From the weather systems to the stars and constellations

in their entirety. From dawn to dusk and from the birth of babies to the birth of the smallest animals. Everything under heaven belongs to God.

I find that God uses different places to meet with me in different ways. Sometimes it is only a few metres from a quiet country road, other times it is in more remote locations. I remember a conversation I had with a seismologist, a man who had spent much of his life in remote corners of the world measuring earthquake activity. He explained that the further from society a seismograph could be placed the better. The reason for this is that society gives out a constant pulse that echoes through the ground. And for a similar reason the further from the distractions of society we can get, then the better we will find the peace of God. With each step our pulse beats more to the rhythm of the creation around us rather than the society we have just left.

I have also found that upward movement adds another dimension. Personally, I have found times upon mountains and hills to be some of the most impressive and spiritually-fulfilling areas of wilderness. Getting up high allows a wider perspective, and enables you to look back down on your life from above. It reminds us of how small we are; yet because we are with God and because of His love, we are significant. We can stand on a hilltop and look out over a vast creation that our God has created.

Biblically we see a variety of wilderness sites being used for spiritual growth. There are flat areas for example, when Isaac spends time in a field meditating (Genesis 24:63). Then there are the forty-year wanderings of the Israelites through the flat desert wilderness. Moving higher, we come to the Mount of Olives at just three and a half kilometres long and rising only sixty metres above the Kidron Valley. In this spot we read of Jesus' regular visits, and the last just before he was arrested and taken to be crucified. Onto the slopes of Mount Carmel standing at just 1742 feet above the Mediterranean Sea. This time it is Elijah, looking out and seeing a cloud the size of a man's hand, as God had promised. On these same slopes Elijah stood alone in front of 450 prophets of Baal and challenged them to follow the living God, who revealed Himself through fire (1 Kings:16-45). Higher still, to the summit of Mount Nebo or Pisgah at 4000 feet and we see Moses meeting with God and being shown the Promised Land just before his death. Higher again and there is Moses having some spectacular meetings with God upon the high rocky slopes of Mount Sinai standing at 7400 feet*. With Jesus there are also times spent upon high mountains, for example, the Transfiguration possibly on the slopes of Mount Hermon rising to over 9000 feet at its highest point. These are just snap-shots of some of the types of wilderness that were spiritually significant throughout the bible, and as we can see it ranges from some of the highest heights to the lowest flatland areas. The things they share is that they are away from towns, roads and buildings.

Wilderness can in some ways be viewed as the opposite to cities or towns. It is into these contrasting places that we should take ourselves, in order to be freed, for a time, from all the limitations and negative influences of the town and city. Jesus wants us to be *in* the world but not *of* the world. Sometimes we feel too at home in the world because we spend too much time surrounded by man-made structures and society with all its hustle and bustle. When we become too at home there, we increase the risk of becoming *of* the world. We need a break from it; we need some time in the wilderness.

Just down the lane and along a minor back road from where I used to live was a little glade, which I found perfect for regular visits and prayer and praise. It's only about fifty meters across and a hundred or so meters long. It is a little cleft between two cornfields with sides too steep for agricultural use. The steeper banks are covered in tall pines and the flatter area in the middle has a blanket of marsh

---

* There is some debate as to whether Horeb and Sinai are the same place, or distinct parts of a similar area. Traditionally Mount Horeb has been seen as a peak named ' Ras es Safaf', meaning 'Willow Peak' and standing 6500ft high. Mount Sinai has been seen as a peak named 'Jebel Musa' meaning 'Mountain of Moses' and standing 7400ft high.

grasses, cut in half by a little burn. The whole site is only minutes from the road and yet it was a place where I definitely felt I was in God's wild creation. It was a place where I could pray with my eyes open, or read His word on a drier day and feel I was surrounded by Him. Now that I have moved back into town I have found a similar site for regular use on my way to work. By taking a short detour I can stop at a little loch and there in a pocket of wildness I can regularly meet with God. I spend time sitting at the water's edge praying, praising, pondering, meditating, writing or simply waiting on God.

At times I have sat at this loch when there has not been a ripple. The water like glass and the reflection as detailed as the scene it mirrors. Sycamore, Beech, Ash and Hawthorn line the banks. At the water's edge – rushes and tall reeds and marsh grasses stand tall and still. A large dead Elm with its leafless branches contrasts against the green life all around it. I have seen the trunk and branches of this old tree lit by the sun's rays as it rises over the horizon to the south-east, when behind it there has loomed an ominous cloud almost black in its density. The old tree has looked as though it glowed. It should be nothing more than a dead leafless skeleton, but reflecting the powerful rays of the sun, and set against the black backdrop, it has looked stunning, as though it emits a light of its own. I have walked through the rest of the day with that image in my mind and the realisation that I, as a Christian, should be glowing, set apart from a darkened world, as I reflect the glory of God. Fields behind the trees, where sheep and cows graze, rise gently up and away from the loch. Sometimes the stillness and the silence is broken by a fish jumping for a fly or the swans and their cygnets swimming leisurely past. Peaceful scenes. Peace that flows into me and fills me like the burns that fill the loch. There is no better way to start the day!

At other times the westerly wind howls across the loch. It is a wind that carries the rain in from the ocean, smelling fresh and bringing the life-giving water that makes this Celtic land so vividly green and diverse. At times I have knelt there at the edge of the water and asked God to fill me with the same life, passion and power so that I could be vivid, a light unto the world. There in the rain, with water dripping down my face, I have started the day by handing it to God, asking Him to be with me, and He always answers. What a way to start the day!

Then other times I have stopped the car and stepped out into a world transformed. Diverse natural colour has been replaced with a monochrome blanket of snow and ice. The whole colourful scene is transformed into one of transparent detail and fragile beauty. Every flake of snow is unique. Each one so delicate that the heat of my breath could destroy it. Yet together these tiny delicate structures have the power to transform the earth over distances and time scales that man could never match. The water is still, locked below its icy crust. No branches quiver under their new coat of ice. Noise seems to be absorbed and dampened by the snow and as I stop walking, silence greets my ears like a most welcome and soothing tune. Stillness infuses my being and my mind, and I find myself simply waiting on God. The car is only a few hundred metres away and yet I stand in the midst of a beautiful white, wild creation. On my previous visit I noticed that someone had dumped some rubbish by the roadside. The gaudy coloured packaging and bent rusting appliances had contrasted harshly with the natural beauty of the surrounding scene. Now I looked and all I could see was a mound of snow. The rubbish was covered. Jesus died on the cross and rose again. I acknowledged Him as Saviour, and asked forgiveness. My sin is covered. The rubbish is covered and I am restored. I was only metres from the road. I was doing no more than simply waiting on and anticipating the presence of God. Sitting in stillness and enjoying the beauty of my Father's creation. Yet in that place long-known truths struck me in profound ways.

This place changes with each visit. It is not high, or remote, but it is wild - a little corner of wild creation where my relationship with God has regularly been developed and strengthened, and where I have found intimacy with Him. I have been able to integrate into my week, times with God at this site, so that wilderness spiritual experiences have become a regular and anticipated part of my relationship with Him. It is like my version of the Mount of Olives, a place that is accessible enough for regular visits.

At the other end of the scale are my own wild walks. Leaving behind society and friends and family and heading for remote corners where few feet go. On these trips I often feel I come back changed. I feel energised. I feel like I have a clearer vision of where I am headed in life. I feel real. After one memorable occasion I was left with the feeling that I had just returned from spending time on holy ground, as though I had been in a temple for two days. I suppose I had - the biggest temple of all with its pillars and paintings, music and halls created by God Himself. These experiences help me imagine what it would have been like for Moses on Sinai or even Jesus on Hermon*. They are times when I meet with God in such a powerful way that my life is transformed, changed from that point on.

These are the wild places I refer to. God's own temples. His wild creation with which He is pleased whether big or small, high or low. The place we know He has full control over. Who can cause the ravens to bring food or manna to appear with the dew? Who can create dry paths through water or calm its rough stormy surface. Who can make whole mountains shake or can whisper through gentle breezes? Who can walk on water? Who can cause massive catches of fish when experienced fishermen can catch none? We know the answer is our living God.

The geographical wilderness is the place in which I have found many of my most-real and thus most-valued spiritual experiences. It is always good to hear from God, and He regularly speaks to us through His word, and His people, and the situations we find ourselves in throughout our day, but nothing can substitute hearing directly from Him for ourselves. Psalm 19 says: 'The heavens declare the glory of God, the skies proclaim the works of His hands'. But how much better it is to sit in some wild place with our face

---

* Hermon comes from a Hebrew word 'ker-mone', which means 'abrupt'. This abrupt slope stretches for almost thirty-two kilometres and has three main peaks, which are often snow-capped.

turned to the vast skies above and see that glory, and know what is proclaimed rather than just read about it or hear about it secondhand. We can stand in awe of our Creator God with the hairs down the back of our neck standing on end and goose-bumps all over as we experience it firsthand.

The wild site is a perfect place for hearing from God. It is a place where all we have heard about Him moves from the head to the heart. A place where God speaks directly into our lives. When we visit someone's house, we learn a lot about them through seeing their home. Their choice of decor, furniture and bits and pieces they have collected over the years tells a story about them and reveals something of their character.

Similarly in the wild site. We step into a place that God has decorated, and it reveals His character. When I look to God's creation and allow Him to reveal His qualities, desires, and love for me through it then the experience is wholly positive. Once you taste of this wilderness spirituality I'm sure you will desire more. You will long to spend time with God in His wild temple as often as you possibly can. These are places in which we can come through a spiritual dry period to find the Promised Land. These are the places where we see the order and balance and harmony of God's creation, and realise again the love He has for us. Once experienced in this way 'wilderness' will stir images of a place of excitement and of spiritual fulfilment. Images of a place where you know that God will meet with you in a radical and intimate way. In wild places we can meet with God and be transformed.

His Nature In His Nature
(Don't Just Sing About It)

"The Beauties of nature are really emanations or
shadows of the excellencies of the Son of God"
(Jonathan Edwards 1703 - 1758)

Creation is an outpouring of God's character; it is a
creative expression of His goodness, His glory, His
divine power and eternal nature. Creation clearly
reflects God's character, yet it is a reflection that can be and
is often missed or misinterpreted. I have read many books
about mountaineering and wilderness adventures, about
travels to remote places, about plants and trees, geology and
nature. The shelves in bookshops and libraries are piled high
with books whose central theme revolves around the natural
world. These books are the products of millions of hours that
have been spent appreciating, studying, contemplating,
experimenting with, playing within, exploring, mapping,
and 'conquering' wild landscapes. So many lives spent
furthering mans knowledge of what surrounds him, yet
what waste, if all that is seen are the individual elements

that make up the whole. If all that is seen is the rock, the water, the earth, the ice, the animal life or plant life; it is like looking at a mirror and seeing only the glass and focusing so closely on it that the reflection itself is missed.

Consider the starry creation stretching out infinitely, clearly visible on a cloudless night. Consider a huge piece of rock, or a hill or mountain, and the mind-blowing timescales involved for it to reach that size and shape. Compared to the vastness of creation we are but mere specks and were it not for love and grace so freely given, we would be utterly insignificant. The only thing that makes us significant in such spatial and timeless immensity is the fact that God, who is bigger and more lasting than these things, loves each one of us. In light of this truth the only thing of worth that we can do is love God in return and worship Him with all our life. This is our place and our purpose, and it is a message we should be compelled to share. Gazing at His wild creation is like seeing a reflection of what we cannot see directly. We see God's character revealed through it and as a result we can understand more about who we are, why we are here and where we are headed. We can all be more aware that while our body roams the earth, a whole unseen spiritual realm surrounds us, and eternity with our loving God stretches out before us. With this realisation, a life of following and worshipping Him can be the only response. Some of that worship must be through meeting with Him and getting to know Him more through what He has made. We must spend time looking into the mirror of His wild creation.

In churches around the world many hymns and songs are sung about the aspects of God that are revealed through natural places or elements. So many times we find lyrics containing references to God's wild creation and this has been consistent from the Psalms through to the most contemporary worship songs. Singing with eyes closed, focusing on God through the words, clapping, dancing, raising our hands - or maybe just standing - depending on the denomination! We worship and praise regularly and yet how often do we truly experience what we sing about?

'Your love is amazing, steady and unchanging,
Your love is a mountain firm beneath my feet.'
(Doerksen & Brown, 'Hallelujah!'
[Your Love Is Amazing]2000)

When was the last time you felt a mountain firm
beneath your feet? When was the last time you stood on a
huge piece of granite exposed through the thin layer of soil
and vegetation; a piece of rock so wide that, if it is as deep,
must surely stretch to the earth's core? Have you stood on
rock so old and with an almost eternal feel; rock that seems
to exude feelings of agelessness and that causes you to stop
and ponder how many others have passed that way before
you? Or caused you to consider how many generations and
eras have come and gone before yours? Have you stood in
these places that cause us to really consider how fleeting our
time here on earth is? Have you ever stood on something so
solid and seemingly unchanging; something so secure and so
vast and almost incomprehensible in its dimensions? Have
you ever stood on that mountain firm beneath your feet and
praised God for the permanency of His love and the eternal
life we have stepped into? Have you stood in such a place
and praised Him with your eyes wide open?

'These thousand hills roll on and on,
Footprints of a mighty God,
They bring me to my knees in praise,
Amazing love, amazing grace.'
(Jacob's Trouble, 'These Thousand Hills', 1990)

When did you last stand on top of a hill or mountain and
look at the panorama of hills spreading out in all directions?
Have you ever stood in such a place and surveyed the amazing
scene? Have you ever stood there with cool fresh air blowing
against your face and contemplated God's amazing love and
grace? Have these footprints of His ever brought you to your
knees amongst the heather and rocks or snow in praise?

'Your love, O Lord, reaches to the Heavens,
Your faithfulness to the skies.
Your righteousness is like the mighty mountains,
Your justice like the great deep.'
                              (Psalm 36:5&6)

And what of that view from atop the mighty mountain?
Have you ever looked at it as a place free from the influence
of man, surrounded by air that seems purer, without the
pollution of towns and cities? Have you ever looked upon
the scene and considered it simply as godly: a part of His
creation as yet free from damage caused by man; a place
that seems somehow virtuous and free from sin; a place that
is a reflection of God's righteousness? From there have you
ever looked to the sea far below and imagined the slope on
which you stand continuing at that angle to the very depths
of the earth? So incredibly vast and deep, as is the justice
of God. Even vaster is the infinite space above. Have you
ever considered as you have gazed at that scene that your
inability to grasp that space is a parallel of your inability to
fully grasp God's love and faithfulness?

'Oceans clap their hands,
The trees they wave their branches,
The rivers run with praise.
All creation will praise.'
            (Darrel Evans, 'The Kingdom Song', 1997)

Have you ever looked over rough seas from remote bays
and listened to the thunderous rumble of the tides and
wind and considered that the power you are witnessing is
a fraction of its creators'? Or can you remember lying on
your back among dry autumn leaves, looking at a distant
sky through thousands of frames formed by supporting
branches? The branches that dance and wave to their
creator. The wind that moves them is unseen, but we see
and feel its effects clearly. The Holy Spirit who moves as
we lie there and praise is not seen, but we can certainly

feel the effects of His presence as He councels, convicts and comforts.

> 'The Ocean is growing,
> The tide is coming in - Here it is,
> Here is our King, Here is our love,
> Here is our God who's come to bring us back to
> Him,
> He is the One, He is Jesus'.
>   (David Crowder Band, 'Here Is Our King', 2005)

When did you last stand and look out over the vast expanse of the Ocean? Have you stood there as the tide comes in, as wave after wave leave meandering line-patterns in the sand? Have you stood and listened to the sound of gentle waves rolling over pebbles, or watched storm-driven waves crash with unstoppable fury against the land? Have you stood with your toes in the tide and your gaze on the distant curving horizon? Have you stood there and thought about just how vast the love of God must be for Him to send His son? What vast love brought the King of Kings here in humility to die on our behalf? A love so vast that it engulfed everything, washed over everything, covered everything, like the tide rising over the shoreline. Have you stood there looking out over the rising tide and praised your King? Has the wind carried His name from your lips and out over the water?

> 'Were the whole realm of nature mine,
> That were an offering far too small'
>   (Isaac Watts, Public Domain)

When was the last time you sat still and meditated on the awesome works of God? When was the last time you set aside time simply to consider how vast and complex and diverse and perfectly balanced the whole realm of natural creation is? I have had images of wild places flood into my mind when I have sung this song. I have imagined that I own them and all the other wild places around them. Then, while thinking of the sacrifice Jesus made for me, I have sung these lines. The words choke in my throat as I realise that even if this vast realm were mine, still it would not be enough to offer in return for what has been done for me.

So if these hymns and songs are worth singing at all then they must be worth singing and meaning every word as fully as we possibly can. There can be an extended dimension to our worship. We do not have to simply imagine, but instead we can reminisce, anticipate and genuinely know why we close our eyes and sing these words.

Give me a day and I will use it to dance. I will spend it offering my praise through thoughts and words and the movements of my body to God. I will move in the freedom bought for me by Christ, and in response to the Holy Spirit flowing through me. I will synchronise my movement to the surrounding environment and in relation to the feelings of joy and excitement within. Joy and excitement needs an outlet. Dance will be the result.

In freedom and filled with joy I will dance from boulder to boulder along a river that runs with praise. Excitedly I will move through trackless valleys. I will spring over fallen trees, twisting and turning, ducking and jumping...over... under...brushing through trees. Trees with their clapping branches. In freedom I will balance on logs and stones, not caring how I look. Standing on one leg, then the other, arms flailing wildly to maintain my balance, mouth spread in a wild smile all the while. Spinning, twisting, jumping... the dance of the wild.

Every part of my body will be in motion as I hop up heather-clad slopes. As I take high steps over the long heather clumps, occasionally staggering and tumbling in excitement. Sweating, panting, I will be energized by a joy within, triggered by my God who is revealed so clearly all around. Bonds will break so the dance of the wild will be danced in full. Safety consciousness and physical demands will be overwhelmed by the pleasure of movement through God's wild creation. Through such movement and filled with awe I will praise Him. I will say 'this place declares

Your glory. This place proclaims the works of Your hands.'
And so onward I will dance. Ever twisting and hopping and
scrambling higher and higher. Up slopes, over crags, through
heather tufts and among peat hags I will move, hearing what
is declared and seeing what is proclaimed. All the while I
will add my own declarations of truth and awe and wonder
and praise. I will not care how I look, as sweat drips from
my forehead. I will think nothing of my dishevelled hair, my
mud spattered, sun-faded, well-worn clothes. I will care only
about moving and praising as once again I shake off self-
consciousness.

I will travel up more crags, hands grasping, arms pulling
legs pushing, feet gripping. My chest will heave as my lungs
are filled with pure air. My heart will pound as it pushes
blood that carries much needed oxygen to every working
muscle. I will squeeze up gullies and cling to firm holds. I
will peer into chasms and out over the rock faces. I will move
from ledge to ledge on ancient rock as I dance on the oldest
of stages; the great stage of wild creation spot-lit by the sun
and its curtains of thick cloud raised. My only audience is
the Creator of all. For Him I dance to the full.

Moving and jumping, I will dance my way to the summit.
There I will pause, balancing on the highest point. There I
will stand as my spirit soars. On top of the hill with infinite
sky above; on top of the hill with my infinite Father all around
and the Holy Spirit flowing through me.

God desires every one of us to experience Him in a
powerful way. He doesn't simply want us to sing our praise
to Him through parallels, analogies and metaphors of His
greatness when we know them only as abstract notions.
Without having direct experience of such places the words
can soon start to roll out of our mouths without us even
realising what we sing. The real tangible nature that reveals
His character is never far away. Just out of the door, or down
the lane, or along the road, or just across those nearby fields,
in that little woodland near your workplace, in the vast sky
above your head, at the shore of the nearby coast or on the
slopes of that little hill. Applying our memory, excitement,

anticipation, and heart knowledge to our worship gives it the extended dimension, the added ingredient that has the power to transform any worship time into an intensely real and intimate time. God did not just tell Abraham that his descendants would be as numerous as the stars; He took him outside of his tent. There, Abraham looked up and saw the vast array of stars spread out across the sky. Abraham was a man of great faith, but I'm sure in that moment his brow would have wrinkled as he wondered how this was going to be. I wonder how many times after that night Abraham looked to the star strewn skies to have his faith boosted. It was not an abstract notion. It was a real reflection of God's prophecy for his life. God met with Abraham and revealed His plan through His vast creation.

God's desire is for us all to have faith and know Him as Abraham did. His desire is for us to meditate on His works, on His wild creation, and through it know more of Him. God led prophets, kings, and leaders out into the wilderness for this very reason. John the Baptist lived a long time amongst creation, and in that place he grew close enough to God to be known thereafter as the one who would prepare the way for Jesus. We can also see that it was more than a simple preference for wild places that drove John the Baptist into the desert, for in the book of Isaiah this "voice from the desert" (Isaiah 40:3) is prophesied many years prior to John's birth. It was God's desire for John to live and grow close to Him in the desert. He planned to do it in this way. His plan was for John to live away from society and draw so close to the Creator that he would be able to prepare the way for the coming King. And he was able to learn of God's character through life lived away from worldly distraction, and instead surrounded by what God has made. In doing so he was sensitive to what God was about to do. A whole life lived in the wild, eating locusts and honey is an extreme calling that few people are given. But even a short time set aside each week to meet with God in some quiet natural place where distractions are reduced, will increase our knowledge of Him and help us develop sensitivity to His ways.

It is also interesting to note in the rest of Isaiah's

prophecy that John's role would be to tame the wilderness, with "mountains levelled and valleys raised up" (Isaiah 40). What is interesting is that being out and living in the wild, set apart from society it seems that John was able to see how unprepared people were for the arrival of Jesus. It was *society* he viewed as wild and unruly and it was *society* that he needed to prepare. In Matthew's account we are told that "when he (John) saw many Pharisees and Sadducees coming to where he was baptising, he said to them: 'You brood of vipers! Who warned you to flee from the coming wrath?'" He goes on to warn that they should not rest on their laurels of having Abraham as their father. I wonder if these people who viewed themselves so highly compared to those around them were in fact the mountains John was told to level. He also treated the poor and the rich equally; could this have been him preparing the way for the least - 'the valleys', to be raised up by Jesus? By living amidst nature and living off nature John knew God's Nature. He knew that the one who would come would not bow to social airs and graces or self-imposed authority. He knew that the one who would come would offer life to all.

Natural places impact all our senses. Many times I have been struck with thoughts or convictions that seem so profound that I have to write them down. Yet if any one else were to read them, they would seem like basic Christian teaching and simple truths. The impact natural places can have on us is that these change from head knowledge to heart knowledge and with that shift come the feelings that make it profound. I remember sitting on a rock by the river high in Scotland's beautiful Glen Nevis. I prayed that the Holy Spirit would fill the valley from the distant peaks to the river bed and as I sat there praying with my eyes wide open, staring, absorbing, and enjoying the surrounding wild beauty I was impacted with a strong sense of praise for God. I wrote:

Awesome. Awesome are these pebbles and rocks I rest upon, broken down and made smooth over time-scales beyond my grasp. Awesome is the waterfall roaring down the slabs, falling hundreds of feet to this valley floor. Awesome are the trees clinging to the valley sides. Slopes so steep they are almost inaccessible yet are carpeted with life. Awesome are the mountains, their slopes huge, elegant, beautiful, pulling my eye toward their summits and to heaven beyond. Awesome are you my God, The Great Creator of all I see, the Great Creator of all that surrounds me. The Great Creator and Father to me.

Unfathomable. Unfathomable are the countless leaves on the countless trees, which bring shade upon shade and waves of praise to you. Unfathomable as the years over which this river has cut its course, from the summit slopes to the open sea via these pools so deep and inviting. Unfathomable is the glacial force that has shaped this valley, these mountains, and this land. Unfathomable are the great depths of the open sea to which this water flows. Unfathomable is Your love o God. Though I know You more each day, still I will have more to learn throughout eternity.

Unique. Unique is every blade of grass on this carpet of green. Unique is every pebble and stone, shaped and smoothed by the flowing water. Unique is every leaf on every branch of the ancient forests rising up the slopes. Unique is every valley and every peak across this beautiful Celtic land. Unique is every person who has trodden this remote path. Over decades and centuries people have come and gone. For every one of them two paths stretch before them. The path that leads to an empty barren place. Or the path that leads to the most beautiful, rewarding and purpose-filled life imaginable. This is the path of following You and the great love and unique plan You have for each of us. It is the path that eventually leads to a place where the valley tracks are paved with gold. Unique are You my God, and the powerful love You have.

This struck me with such force that my hands shook as I wrote and tears ran down my face. Nothing new. Nothing I hadn't heard or read before. But what made it so profound was the new depth I had in my belief of who God is and how much He loves me. On scraps of paper and in notebooks and diaries I have countless pieces of writing like this, scribbled down hastily as some aspect of scripture, or some aspect of God's character has become more real to me.

> "One thing I ask of the Lord, this is what I seek: that
> I may dwell in the house of the Lord all the days of
> my life, to gaze upon the beauty of the Lord and to
> seek him in his temple"
>
> (Psalm 27:4)

The beauty of the Lord is something I feel I have only begun to understand through contemplating His wild creation. When I sing about or think about His beauty, I find my mind flooded with images of places I have been and things I have seen. Tall pines reaching to heaven. Rivers of the purest, clearest water pouring over smooth rocks and reflecting blue skies above. Sunsets seen from high on a mountain where for just a brief moment the world turns a shade of pink, or sunrises seen from on high as the first rays of daylight strike the high snows and set them ablaze with colour. They are all memories of beauty, firmly lodged in my mind so that when I hear mention of the beauty of the Lord, it is these memories that bring understanding: memories of revelation through the physical wilderness.

At one level this is simply the beauty of creation, yet at another it is the beauty of the Creator Himself. When God reveals Himself to Moses, it is qualities of His character that he sees. The goodness and glory of God pass before him. In 'Exodus' we read, "No man can see the face of God and live" (Exodus 33 :20). Like Moses we get a glimpse of God's glory through His qualities that are revealed through His creation. The colours, the shapes, and diversity of our surroundings would be empty visual stimulation if it did not reveal something infinitely deeper. Do so many thousands of people paint, study, meditate on and write about the natural world, or is it not that they try to capture and understand 'something deeper'? "To gaze upon the beauty of the Lord and seek him in his temple," – one day we will be able to gaze directly upon the beauty of the Lord and live. By drawing close to God and living more fully for Him, we too can reflect His beauty and character. We were created in His likeness and because of Jesus we have been given a second chance to be restored to that former position. We can, once again, stride powerfully through life being an example of the restoring power of God, rather than shuffling about in darkness.

Scots-born founder of Yosemite national park in California, John Muir, is an example of the powerful impact wild places can have on life. He lived an incredible life, in which he saw the beauty in nature and spoke and wrote so passionately about it that he has gone down in history as the 'father of conservation' and the 'greatest wilderness evangelist'. Born and raised in a strict Calvinist home in Scotland in 1838, Muir was forced to memorise Scripture. The penalty for failure was the whip. Under this threat he memorised the whole of the New Testament and much of the Old Testament too. He would find himself memorising scripture about his heavenly Father's unfailing love knowing that his earthly father would lash him if he got it wrong. Upon leaving the mist and the heather of Scotland, he journeyed to California. There among the granite, sun and Giant Sequoia trees he realised that the inconsistency lay in man and not God. Near the end of His life, while at a farm in Wisconsin, he wrote of the first taste of American wilderness when he had first arrived with his family -

> "This sudden splash into pure wildness... how utterly happy it made us! Nature streaming into us, wooingly teaching her wonderful glowing lessons, so unlike the dismal grammar ashes and cinders so long thrashed into us. Here, without knowing it, we were still at school; every lesson a love lesson, not whipped but charmed into us."
>
> (John Muir, 'My First Summer in Sierra')

Many people have studied the life of this great Scot and debate continues as to whether he drew close to God through the wild or the wild itself became his god. One thing is certain though, among the forests, valleys, alpine meadows and mountains, John Muir found a place where all that memorised scripture was surrounded by consistency rather than hypocrisy. In the wild, God's consistent and loving character is powerfully revealed. That God sent His only son to die for us seems more comprehensible in a place of order, balance and diversity, than amidst man's world of unrest, inequality, and bland expectation. To gaze upon nature with all it's ordered diversity and detail and find Christ revealed in all his constant loving glory surely is a beautiful thing. It is so beautiful that for many of us we could have our relationship with Him radically transformed, when all the negative things that have influenced our image of Him (however well meaning) are stripped away. Stripped away by the revealing power of God's creation. Stripped away by His beauty shining through it.

Mystery is another hugely appealing aspect of the wild, and another ingredient that adds to the beauty of such situations. We long to know what is beyond the next peak, round the next corner, across the river, at the other side of the forest. We seek answers as to how and why things grow, where life comes from, where we come from, what our purpose is. We have been created with an inquisitive nature. Gaze upon wild creation and the mysteries held there and some of this need for answers is somehow dissipated. We know that we cannot explore every crack and crevasse. We know we cannot walk the length of every valley. We look to the skies and know that our mind cannot grasp the fact that it goes on forever. Infinity is beyond our comprehension, but we know it is real. Amidst wild places we can somehow accept that our finite minds will never fully understand the infinite mind of God. In such a way God remains a mystery. He will always be intriguing, exciting, alluring, and mysterious. There will always be more to know and discover and more layers to uncover.

Surely one of the greatest mysteries of our God is that He loves us so much that He sent His Son to die and pay the price so that we may live. When we accept that, we also must accept that our frantic lives are only the surface of something infinitely deeper called eternity. The realisation or revelation of this bigger picture brings freedom to life. Living in the here and now immediacy of society to the neglect of all else, is like splashing about in a shallow lukewarm pool that has become cut off from the river. Accepting Jesus as Saviour is like plunging back into the deep moving water of the river. Its cold waters shock our bodies into life and out of the lethargy that results from the shallows. It is a reality check. Our eyes are opened to the deeper truth that surrounds our life. But in a life surrounded by worldliness, we can find ourselves drifting again towards the lukewarm shallows. Immersing ourselves in the natural creation of our Father can have us once again pushing out into the deep. For a life of effectiveness we need to regularly plunge into the deeper pools and think about this bigger picture. Places where we glimpse the deep that surrounds us, the deep love of God.

> "I pray that out of his glorious riches he may strengthen you with power through His Spirit in your inner being, so that Christ may dwell in your hearts through faith. And I pray that you, being rooted and established in love, may have the power, together with all the saints, to grasp how wide and long and deep is the love of Christ"
>
> (Ephesians 3:16-18).

Goodness, mercy, love, kindness, righteousness, glory, and the eternal. All these aspects of God and many more besides are revealed through His wild creation and make it an incredibly beautiful place. God did not create and then step back from His creation. He continues to be in control of it and reveal Himself through it. Renowned mountaineer of the early 1900's F.S. Smythe suggests eloquently that every day at sunrise we can witness God's ongoing control of His creation. He writes that:

> "The light came slowly and with incredible stealth. It was poured slowly, lingeringly and lovingly into the world, like the most precious of celestial liquids.

First of all the snow we trod was revealed. We had seen it before, wan in the starlight, but now it took on a bolder tone. Objects hitherto unseen or only guessed at became visible. Very slowly the peaks separated themselves from the night. Against the stars they were merely irregular wedges of darkness, and lost in the darker regions of the sky; but light revealed them as solid and substantial. Their change from darkness to light, from two dimensioned to three dimensioned form and solidity, was extraordinarily subtle, an imperceptible yet regular rhythm of transmutation. In just such a way must God have given light to the world, not in an instant, but gradually and with ever increasing power and love. And, that mankind shall not forget the miracle, a lesser miracle is performed daily, that, like some new truth, steals unsuspected upon the world."

(F.S. Smythe, 'The Spirit of the Hills')

I have had the pleasure and the privilege of standing on snowy ridges and summits to watch this daily miracle. I have stood trembling as God, pouring into me in increasing power and love, has impacted my emotions, my mind and my body. It is an experience available to all, yet one that is missed by many.

I have felt a similar sense of awe during springtime, when all the buds form and hang ready to burst into vivid green. That time of year when there is a crisp clarity in the air, when you get that lifting feeling that summer is just around the corner. While the trees and shrubs stand bare it is hard to imagine the world with so much more green, and yet spring comes and an incredible energy can be felt. Then gradually the energy flows and the buds burst and with the colour come fragrance, and feeling and the anticipated wonder of life. Like the first light of day it comes not with a bang but with a gradual transforming rhythm. A true miracle of new life made plain every year. It rises from the dark earth that has been locked in frost and grows and transforms the world. Like our Saviour, who rose from death and out of the darkness of the tomb to reveal Himself to many and offer hope and life to all who turn to Him.

On the hillside stands a lonely Pine, its needles pointing skyward. Pointing from branches that move and sway, conducted by an invisible wind. Its branches wave while its roots delve into the earth, reaching almost to the nearby burn. Fresh clear water cascades over rocks and plunges into pools. Endlessly it flows from summit heights toward the vast expanse of the sea. There, fathoms and leagues of water cover the earth, made up of innumerable single droplets. Like the droplet hanging there on the pine needle on the end of the branch that reaches out over the burn. A droplet of water that has come from the clouds above, and before that from the sea. There it hangs briefly, poised to drop. There it hangs reflecting a whole world of colour. There it hangs, then it falls, into the moving water and off it goes joining the rest of the moving water toward the deep expanse of the ocean. This is a natural world in motion. Continual motion, all linked together. It has been intimately woven together stitch by stitch, to form a vast tapestry of life. It is no tangled mess of thread randomly flung together. Each stitch is supported by another, and at the same time supports another. This is an ordered creation. It is diverse and wild and vast but it is fully ordered and reflects the Creator whose hands continue to hold it in place. This is a beautiful creation, knit together by a God of love. I meditate on His works, and in doing so I fulfil an act of worship and praise.

My God your love is real, like this hillside. So vast like the deepest of seas beyond the shores. So immense and eternal like the sky viewed at night. You bring peace like the calm that stills the surface of a loch. You are fiercely powerful beyond even the wildest of storms. My Father once again I have left the distractions and distortions of society behind. Like John the Baptist, Your voice from the desert, I now immerse myself in your wild creation. In this place I learn more of You and Your ways. In Your likeness man has been created. In Your likeness I have been created. I long to live my life fully for you. You are the awesome God, Creator of all. I bow before no other. I long to grow more sensitive to You, and to know You more fully each day. You are the awesome God, Creator of all, Author of life.

Holy Spirit I cannot see You, yet I know You are here. Once again I feel You stirring my emotions, revealing and convicting and caring. Once again sitting here in Your presence, I feel the compelling desire to call others out into these places. That they can see the works of God, to meditate on them, and worship Him through doing so. I thank You for the intimacy You bring to this living relationship, intimacy made possible through the sacrifice of Jesus.

Lord Jesus, I thank You that You have formed a bridge between man and God. Thank You that the cross forms a bridge over the deepest ravine so that I can kneel before my Father. You are the greatest hero to have ever walked this earth. My desire is to live in Your likeness, to emulate Your perfect life. I fall short always, but great is the mercy and grace that flows from God. Jesus, just like You I walk in wild places. Just like You I surround myself by my Father's wild creation and in that place I meet with Him. You, the Son of God, came to earth and made this possible. Thank You my King.

I pray many more voices could join with the roar of rivers running with praise and that many more hands would rise to You like the branches. I thank You that living like this feels like life lived to its fullest. You are the awesome Creator of all.

At Risk Without Risk

'But risk we must, because the greatest hazard in life
is to risk nothing. The man, the woman, who risks
nothing does nothing, has nothing, is nothing.'

(Anonymous)

*The burn flows slowly by, following a meandering course
as we sit with our backs against the valley side. The deep
heather is as comfortable as any armchair. Great rays
of sunlight flood into the valley creating a welcome lazy heat.
Peace has infused itself into every individual in the group.
This hill walking group for adults with learning difficulties
usually involves an excited and often noisy lunch time as the
participants chat and laugh, no longer restrained by any of
the usual social expectations. Today there is silence. Just the
subtle tune composed of the trickling burn, the occasional
buzz of an insect drifting past and distant Lark song as they
rise above the heather.*

*Looking along the row of smiling faces I see each exuding
the joys found in these wild places. Every week, and with every
visit to such places, more memories are made. Memories of
exploration, challenges and adventure and of all the positive
emotions that are stirred as a result. And today... memories
of a sunny day and a deep peace. I look along the row of*

relaxed bodies cushioned by the heather and long grasses and find myself thinking about the pile of risk assessment forms littering my desk back in the office. There are so many procedures to follow and forms to fill in that the place of these wild walks on our weekly programme seems to be continually in question. It seems close, sometimes, that these experiences will be lost for those in the group, that these days of peacefulness amidst the wilderness will be confined to the memories of these hill walkers with their smiling faces.

I lie back in the warmth of the sun and let my eyes be drawn up gullies and over crags, then sweep down the slopes to rest on forests, then old dry-stone walls, then the nearby burn. Then they drift back up from the burn absorbing the scene before me. They are drawn up the slope that rises steeply across the other side of the narrow valley. They follow along the remains of an old wall full of gaps where the stones lie low and moss clings to their grain. A swathe of bracken streaming out across the hillside carries my gaze to a small waterfall cascading into an unseen pool. Distance means its flow is silent to my ears. Above it my eyes roam its course up toward the huge corrie from where it springs. Above the corrie walls stands the summit with a backdrop of blue infinity. From there I would see the summits of the other hills and mountains that make up this wild Scottish Land. Each one with a Celtic name and character all of its own. Each one distant - as distant as my office desk now seems. I stretch and breathe deeply, and smile like those around me.

We live in an age almost obsessed with risk avoidance. A widespread fear of claims and lawsuits amongst employers and those providing public services means risk assessment and minimisation is a workplace and social priority. Many sociologists comment that in Britain, like most countries, there is a major negative impact on our society as a result of possible litigation when accidents occur. The term 'Nanny State' has been applied by many of those who are critical of this minimal risk culture. It is a culture that means tasks, practices and environments have undergone a phase of rapid change so that risk assessments can be carried out and the required changes be made. More importantly, mindsets have changed, and the effects are not entirely positive. My colleagues and I are employed to develop and run a programme of sporting activities specifically for adults with learning disabilities. We, along with the project manager, regularly find ourselves defending the place of many outdoor activities on our program. Continually we have to fill out forms, and attend meetings to satisfy concerns over the safety of these activities. More injuries have occurred during the team sports we play in games halls, yet it is exploration, orienteering, and hill walking groups that we most regularly find ourselves defending. Risk is present in wild places, but risk is present in all places, in all activities. Risk is present through simply living life. The smiling faces of the participants in our outdoor activities, the tales of adventure they go home eager to tell their peers, parents and carers, the sense of achievement they have when they can look at the top of a distant hill and say "I've been up there": that is proof that any small risk involved in being there is far outweighed by the benefits.

> 'The risk faced by not getting out alone into wild places far outweighs the risk entailed in being there'.
>
> (William Plunkett)

What benefits are being lost through risk minimisation going too far? What about walking along tracks and trails, away from safety-obsessed societies and into wild free places; how many people now enjoy the thrill of travelling alone, on foot into such places? How many people now experience real wild adventure and live life in the freedom that has been bought for us? How many people take faith-based risks and see their whole Christian life as an adventure to be lived to the full? How many now prefer to read about adventure or watch programmes and films about it?

The media have and will continue to portray wild activities, and particularly mountaineering and hill walking, in a way that exaggerates the risk involved. Why? Because they are popular stories, and they sell newspapers and boost ratings, particularly when sensationalised. I am in no way advocating extreme sports here. This is not a call to go bungee jumping or skydiving or swimming with sharks. There is no call here to be extreme and there is no need to participate in extreme pursuits to enjoy adventure. People love adventure, whether it is in books films or tales. They seem to be regarded with a certain fascination, perhaps due to an underlying desire for a personal role in such an experience, a deep longing to be a part of something bigger than the comfy, safe, mundane world around us. Simply walking in a wild place can be an adventure, but often the risk is not as high as the sensationalised stories in the press and other media would have us believe, particularly when common sense is used in such places. Joe Simpson became well known for his adventure, captured in his book and subsequent film 'Touching the Void', which involved falling down a mountain in a remote part of Chile. He states that statistically each year in Britain there are more people killed fishing than mountaineering. We do not, however, perceive fishing with the same degree of caution. Why not? Simpson suggests that someone falling off a mountain makes a more marketable article than someone slipping into a river!

Sweat pours down my face. It stings my eyes and drips from my nose. My water bottle has been empty for hours as I move through this summer heat. The sun continues to beat down on my head now throbbing slightly from dehydration. Uphill and down I have moved while fluid is lost from my body and with it my energy is sapped, and now I feel as though the reservoirs of both are running dry. Water shortage in the Scottish hills is a rare experience, and not a pleasant one. My head feels fuzzy and my tongue sticks to the inside of my mouth. Even the rocks I walk over look dusty and in need of water. Plants look tired and wilted. Plants are looking like how I feel.

Stumbling legs carry me jarringly along the ridge until a point where it narrows and the ground drops steeply to either side, to valley floors below. In one of these valleys I can see a river cutting its course through peaty ground. The sides are too steep here to climb down unroped. I walk along the edge and see a waterfall pouring out of the higher rocks on the opposite valley side. It falls onto the rocks below and sprays out in all directions. Fresh clear water that I long for. I carry on until a point where the valley side eases in angle, but only slightly. It is still steep. It is steep enough that a slip or tumble would see that I do not stop until I reach the spray-dampened rocks far below. I know I need to replenish the water that has been lost through sweat and motion. I need to fill the reservoirs that have been rapidly drained. I long to plunge my face into the clear water and feel its coolness flood my body as I gulp it down.

Cautiously I commit myself to the descent. Each foothold is tried and tested while my hands grip anything that will take my weight. Down and down, sun-warmed rock by sun-warmed rock. Down until I reach the trees that cling to the valley side. While my feet edge down the slope using sturdy tree-trunks as footholds, my hands use branches and exposed roots as anchors. I take it slowly, every move made carefully until the point where the ground starts to level out. Now my hands are by my side rather than clinging and grasping. Now I stride across the open valley bottom. I unbuckle my pack while I walk, swinging it onto one shoulder, then from there to the ground at the edge of the river. Lying across grass and stone I plunge my face into the river and drink. The water far exceeds any other drink I have ever had. I understand more fully what refreshment means. I feel new energy rise inside. I roll onto my back. High above I can see the ridge and the valley edge where rock faces fall steeply until they meet the trees. The descent had not been as difficult as it had looked from above. Even if it had been though, I would gladly have tried even for a single sip of this fresh cool water.

"O God, you are my God, earnestly I seek you;
My soul thirsts for you, my body longs for you,
in a dry and weary land where there is no water.
I have seen you in the sanctuary

And beheld your power and your Glory.
Because your love is better than Life
My lips will glorify you.
I will praise you as long as I live,
And in your name I will lift up my hands."
(Psalm 63:1-4)

When we are children we love tales of mystery and adventure. When we get older it seems that many of us find these tales no less appealing. Box office figures would reveal that fact, with so many 'epics' becoming the biggest hits. The most popular stories have a hero. The hero is the one who pushes themself further than the rest. They are the one who believe so fully in what they pursue that they will be right there on the front line and would even stand and face the enemy alone. The hero would prefer to die trying rather than give up on a quest so worth pursuing. They do not see settling for a quiet life of comfort as an option. The hero is the one who will in the end be raised as the victor or remembered with respect for giving their all. They are the one covered in injuries. The one whose story will be passed from generation to generation. The hero is the one who sees clearly that any risk or danger involved is insignificant when held in comparison to what can be gained. The hero does not turn away from their quest because it is viewed as too risky. The hero is the one most of us long to be.

Many people have gone down in history as great followers of God - as heroes. The bible is full of examples, and of descriptions of the dangers they faced: a passage through parted seas, a divine meeting high on mountains that tremble and smoke, being thrown into lions' dens, fights with giants, standing alone challenging whole nations and exposing their false gods, telling authorities they are wrong, facing storms, shipwrecks, imprisonment, beatings, floggings, martyrdom, persecution. Those who decide to follow God do not find themselves in a life of comfort and ease. There are hardships, risk, danger, and adventure. God allows it but He is always there and makes a way for His people to be victorious. He is glorified through people who

go all out for Him whatever the cost. Those who put their
necks on the line. Those who live the whole of their lives as
an adventure in the knowledge that life eternal stretches
out before them.

Is there not a deep part in us all that wants to be a
radical, wild, follower of God, whatever the cost? Do we not
all desire to follow God so closely that we go down in history
as someone who gave their all to the glory of God, one who
lived a life of purpose and meaning and walked constantly
in light of eternity? Surely we would all opt for a life of
excitement and fulfilment, of satisfaction and adventure.
But then we are surrounded by a society that thinks these
things are best viewed from a distance. So that brief bubbling
over of longing for a part in a wilder more radical life soon
fizzles out as we settle back in our big padded chair to read
of some other wild person's testimony or watch the latest
epic blockbuster. Our dreams are put away in some dusty
recess of our mind, and remembered occasionally as just
some youthful daydream we once had. That wild vision of
a different life becomes as blurred as rain soaked windows.
And so we settle down to a life of mediocrity. But every now
and then there is a stirring within us. A longing for more,
a longing for intimacy with the Creator of all things, our
Father the God of the universe. A life that involves a bit of
risk taking. Risk, in a way, is the essence of faith: to act on
what we cannot see, or know for certain. Yet we act anyway
because we sense it is right, and feel that God is leading us,
and as we do we take a risk. The result is blessing.

My wife and I were discussing this topic of faith and
living the Christian life as an adventure and she stated that
she thought an adventurous life could be summed up as
'immediate obedience to God's voice'. I wish I had thought of
that! With God we know anything can happen, and we really
have little idea what will happen, yet we have the certainty
that we are in safe hands. David heard from God that he
should go and face the giant Goliath. Goliath was "Over nine
feet tall. He had a bronze helmet on his head and wore a
coat of scale armour of bronze weighing about five thousand
shekels" (about 125 pounds or 57 kilograms); "on his legs he

wore bronze greaves, and a bronze javelin was slung on his back. His spear shaft was like a weavers rod and its iron point weighed about five hundred shekels" (about 15 pounds or 7 kilograms), (1 Samuel 17:4-7). Saul and his entire army had spent over forty days listening to the taunts of Goliath each morning, and not one of them would go out to fight him. Then along comes David, a mere shepherd boy, who says to Saul "Let no-one lose heart on account of this Philistine; your servant will go and fight him" (1 Samuel 17:32). David had heard from God and he knew that it was by the power of God that the giant would be defeated and so he was willing to embark on an adventurous and entirely risky act. David is immediately obedient to God's voice. Saul is not, and having at first doubted whether David should be allowed to go out and face the giant, Saul eventually offers David his own armour. It is too big for the boy of course. However, David has heard from God, and so he acts. Out he goes in his own tunic without armour, taking only his staff, his sling and five smooth stones chosen from a burn. If this action had not been a response to God's voice then it would be an act of sheer stupidity or madness. As it stands, David went out and with his first stone the giant fell dead. To live this Christian life as an adventure, we need to have an intimate relationship with our Father. We need to be following his lead with immediate obedience.

I certainly want a life that is full of the excitement and healthy fear that goes hand in hand with risk. Yet at the same time I also seek stability and certainty, comfort, intimacy and safety. Too much of either extreme is dangerous. A life of hearing and obeying the voice of God will bring the balance and we can hear Him by spending time before Him, away from the predictability of daily routines and their inherent distractions. There are adventures lying just off the beaten track that are available to all of us. These adventures that God is calling us to will take us out into His natural creation to meet with Him in a new way. Anything that takes us beyond the confines of everyday routines soon feels like an adventure. In partaking in these experiences we allow ourselves to develop in ways that are free from the negative influences of the social world around us. Slow walks along a meandering burn, exploring woodlands where birds and trees provide the only sights and sounds, footprints left along a sandy shore, long arduous climbs, hair-raising descents, joy of movement over wild terrain and through settings that epitomise tranquillity and others that seem to show only the might and power of their Creator. All these and more have been used by Him to teach me new things and to make me who I am today.

We all can and should live our life fully for Jesus. We can all live a life that we can look back on as a great adventure. Adventures in wild places can help us develop and apply this attitude to the whole of our life. However, there is nothing in these short wild adventures if they are not set in the context of a bigger adventure and applied fully to it. On a wild weekend in Scotland with some friends from my home church, we found a place where we could descend down steep banks to reach the fast flowing river at the bottom of a steep gorge. From above, the river was more audible than visual for it has, over countless years, cut a course deep down into the valley leaving huge boulders wedged between the steep gorge sides. Amongst these boulders - many bigger than houses - are a series of tunnels, caves and holes through which we squeezed until we could see the river flowing through its subterranean caverns. Along passages and through holes we wriggled, pausing to look at how the water has shaped the rocks over time scales beyond our comprehension. We pushed through and climbed over boulders that have long been hidden from daylight. After one particularly difficult section a great shaft of light poured through a gap in the boulders high above. This light revealed the bottom of a slow moving pool. Large round pockets could be seen under the points where water flowed continuously into the pool. If we were to spend a hundred years in that very spot we would see very little change. Yet there they were, all around us, rocks sculpted and being continually changed by the waters flow.

As day became evening and the great mountains all around cast their shadows over the valley we retreated to our mountain hut accommodation and there our conversation was centred upon our experiences out among God's wild creation. One member of the group shared that during the adventure of clambering our way through the tunnels he had come to realise the need to apply this sense of adventure to the whole of his life. He shared with us that too often he would come against a difficulty in life and he would simply back down or try to find a different route. During his time among the boulders he had realised that if he just pushed through the difficulties in life he would enjoy the sense of adventure in the whole of his life, and would also see how God was shaping him through the difficulties. He told us excitedly that he would be returning to an everyday life that would seem different. A life where difficulties would be viewed like those tight spots and awkward moves in the boulder adventure. He would respond to God and push through and as a result he would see the positive shaping that comes through living the whole of his life as an adventure.

Times in wild places with their inherent risk can inspire an adventurous lifestyle. A lifestyle in which we love to speak boldly and compel people to turn to Christ. Closet Christians are the opposite of adventurous, faith-filled followers of Jesus.

> 'You are the light of the world. A city on a hill cannot be hidden. Neither do people light a lamp and put it under a bowl. Instead they put it on its stand, and it gives light to everyone in the house. In the same way, let your light shine before men, that they may see your good deeds and praise your Father in heaven'.
> (Matthew 5:14-16)

We should allow ourselves to be seen; we should be exposed in the confidence of our assured victory. This call for everyone to get out and meet God in His wild creation is not about escaping; it is about seeing our own life in its proper context. It is about getting out there, meeting God and coming back more determined and inspired than ever to change the world - and more convinced that we can. It means living in the certainty of a bigger picture, the certainty of God's plan. The wild site has a definite role to play in that process for through it we can become less preoccupied with self, and more able to see the bigger picture. As we become less preoccupied with self and safety and risk avoidance we can begin to understand who we really are - new creations. Bold adventurous men and women, who are not tied up in the apathetic mundanity of the everyday world. Not afraid to say that Jesus is *the* way. When we do what Jesus did, we live a life of adventure. We keep moving forward no matter what difficulty we face. We keep pushing on knowing that in doing so, and in staying active in our spiritual journey, we remain fully alive. And in remaining fully alive we find that even in the hardest times we can face the hardships and difficulties head on and with praise always on our lips.

I have not always taken a sensible approach to the great outdoors or had the respect for wild places that I should have. In fact it is only by the grace of God that I can write these words! One foolhardy weekend with three friends, as inexperienced as I was, we embarked on a wild adventure. No concern was expressed about the risks involved. Even less thought was given to what equipment we should take. We were like David going to face Goliath without stopping to pick up any stones for his sling!

We crossed over the top of a mountain named Schiehallion in the central highlands. Her usual rocky summit lay under a blanket of snow and ice but it was only thoughts of fun and laughs and the beauty of this high frozen world that filled our minds. We even laughed at the surprised looks of other hill-walkers at the late hour we were setting out! We were of course without crampons and carried not even a single ice-axe among us (the bare essentials of winter walking). The snow was crisp, and on the steepest sections our boots gripped well, giving a feeling of reassurance.

We had dropped down to the bothy at the Southern side of the hill, sliding most of the way on our waterproofs and carry mats. The bothy offered an oasis of relative luxury and shelter from the freezing wilderness. We sat with our backs against dry wood-panelled walls on a wooden floor and talked excitedly about how cut off from the world we were. Out of a small window we could see the snow swirling around. Even inside we had to stay in our sleeping bags, and the bag full of snow we had brought in with us to melt and drink remained as frozen as the land outside. Still, we felt cosy and well at ease with each other.

There were four of us, and each had left a very different life behind for the weekend. Simon laughed and joked with a sense of humour as dry as the wood we lay on. His abrupt statements were, as always, both amusing and puzzling simultaneously, in a positive kind of way. He had previously been nominated student of the year and, at the time, was as deep in fluid engineering equations and formulas as the very seas he studied! He had left his studies behind and now sat in the bothy, as always, ensuring an air of humour and unpredictability was present. He adds vibrancy to any situation and lives life to the full, giving himself completely to anything he deems worthy.

Also with us was Ross, a mystery, simple as that. He moves from country to country, enjoying each one but settling nowhere. Perhaps he is the epitome of wanderlust! He sat in the bothy leaving whatever other country he would otherwise have been in behind him for the weekend. He sat contentedly laughing at Simon's wit, and always adding plenty of his own. And finally Andrew. He did most of the cooking, sitting over the stove making brews of tea and coffee. Always sorting, fixing or adjusting something. Perhaps it is the years of involvement in the Venture Scouts organisation. He is full of drive and ambition and is one of those people who you know is both reliable and honest. He always expresses concern over the steepness of the slope on which we stand or the width of the ridge stretching before us, yet he always moves smoothly and confidently over any obstacle and is often first to stand on an icy summit. He had left his job in a London bank far behind for the weekend. For him, the contrast between where he sat yesterday and where he sat in the remote bothy was greater than any. It is with these three that I have chosen to spend many a wilderness trek. It was these three friends that I spent much of my youth with. They have remained consistent friends throughout most of my life. They have seen the change in me as I handed my life fully over to God. I know that it is a change that can severely alter many a friendship, but thankfully, not ours, or at least only for the better. It is fuel for Andrew's jokes about 'cults', an opportunity for Ross' inquisitive mind, and I think in some ways confirmation to the conclusion that Simon has already come to, that God does exist. As I sat in that bothy staring at our candle I knew that only I left behind a weekend that included church. I knew that only I looked at the surroundings, the white world outside, and saw God revealed so obviously. I knew that this was part of the reason that I felt so torn between enjoying being there and the strong desire to be at home with Lindsay. Only she truly knows me. Only she can tell at a glance how I feel, and shares such a real relationship with God. In the cold bothy we gradually settled for the night. At least we had good sleeping bags, and lay on carry mats. I fell asleep thinking of Lindsay and also wishing that all three of my companions could carry the hope that I carry, and know the Father that I know, and perhaps then they could know even just a little more of who I am.

I awoke in the morning with Andrew's face too close for comfort. I turned onto my back glad that I was cosily tucked between him and Simon, who slept looking smug on my other side. I watched my breath rise with every exhale and swirl about the still air. I wanted to get up but didn't want to wake the others. I always seem to have this problem. While they sleep soundly I was itching to get going and explore the world around. Inevitably I rise first, making our breakfast, packing, then pacing up and down hurrying the others. Simon inevitably looks up at me from the porridge he is still eating and mutters 'standard', referring to this now regular procedure, much to the amusement of the other two. Andrew's rucksack must of course be packed in an approved way. While practicality fills his, haste fills mine so I can offer him little in the way of assistance!

At last we set off and in seemingly no time at all reached

a summit. However, we did not pay much attention to the map so we were not entirely sure on which summit we stood! This added to our concern, as the wind seemed suddenly stronger, and cloud had blown in as fast as our slide down the slopes of Schiehallion the previous night. Rather than descend the longer and narrower ridge we had just climbed, we decided to drop down a more direct route over the broader slopes of the other side. The trouble was that we could not decide which route led to the slope we sought, and there was alarmingly little distinction between snow and sky. I later learned that 'whiteout' is the term for this. I produced the map and compass and handed them quickly to Simon, the engineering wizard, who looked briefly at them, then back at me, and then passed them to Andrew the pragmatic Scout, who with freezing hands passed them straight onto Ross the global traveller. He shrugged his shoulders and stuffed them quickly into his pocket. Off we set, hoping that it was the right direction. None of us had possessed the ability to discern the direction from map and compass. Thankfully it did not take us long to drop below the cloud and regain our bearings. We sat in the snow, all frivolous again but each silently aware of how suddenly out of control the situation had been.

Simon then gave a brief lecture on the efficiency advantages of using gravity and carry mat to take him rapidly down the huge slope, and off he went, disappearing quickly over the edge onto the unknown slopes below. Cliffs? Probably not! The Traveller and Venture Scout heeding the words of Simon detached the carry mats from their rucksacks. I set off plodding quickly down the slope, taking the sensible 'much less efficient' method of descent. Further down the slope I was surprised the other two had not yet sped past. Looking back I saw that the Scout had come up with a better plan and was busy directing preparations for an even more efficient and faster descent utilising an emergency plastic Bivvy bag stuffed with both rucksacks and room for two passengers sitting on top. I continued on down the slope and looked back only when I heard the whoops of delight from way above. Simon below, had stopped and was watching the new higher-speed method with envy.

The descent reached a dangerous speed and simultaneously laughter had ceased and the passengers bailed off, rolling and sliding to a stop just before the slope steepened further. Simon looked on smugly from below, standing before the protruding rocks he had just managed to stop short of - adding to his theory of efficient descent that there comes a point when over-efficiency leads to heightened and unjustifiable risk!

The constructed vehicle increased in speed, orange bivvy bag flapping noisily, snow flurrying out behind it and sounding like the roar of the wind near the summit. In a moment when the subconscious takes over, I found myself running toward the hurtling object. Just as I realised the stupidity of this bizarre action I also realised that it was too late to do anything about it. In a split second my lower legs were hit with such force that I flipped almost 360 degrees. The white world around me spun and went dark. Then silence. I felt the cold snow on my face. I opened my eyes and realised I had been spun right round and lay with my feet pointing up the slope. I watched below as the bag sped past Simon who watched with amusement as it hit the protruding rocks and the contents of the bag and rucksacks scattered in all directions.

The silence was shattered by the guffawing laughter from above and below. I laughed and cried at the same time as pain shot up both legs. In that second I was sure both legs were broken and again I was faced with a very serious situation. Andrew and Ross appeared at my side but did not say or do anything other than bend over almost sick with laughter. I retched, not from laughter but from shock, pain and the position I was lying in with my head lower than the rest of my body. A more composed Andrew slowly slid me round and asked me to move my feet. I couldn't move anything without a lot of pain. I felt extremely cold all of a sudden, but better after sitting up straighter. I looked down the slope and saw Simon glancing up from below as he gathered up the strewn rucksack contents from among the rocks. He later told me that in his mind he was formulating the plan, that they would all try to get me back to the bothy, then one would stay with me while the other two ran back over the miles of wild terrain for help. The now shredded emergency bag wasn't going to be any use to me!

I exercised a controlled slide down to the base of the slope, head-first, while lying on my back, wincing as my legs were shaken about. All three of my friends helped me slowly to my feet and supported me as I slowly put weight on them. The seriousness of the situation was sinking in. I found I could walk very slowly on the level with a lot of support. Eventually this very non-efficient method got us back to the bothy. My legs throbbed as I took my boots off. Simon stated matter-of-factly that they were not broken but probably cracked. I felt sure that after a nights rest and warmth I would be able to make it back out over the white miles between us and the car. Next morning my legs were so swollen that I couldn't lace up my boots properly. However, I could walk with my belongings distributed between the other three and following a level path through the snow that the others prepared ahead of me. To this day I have lumps on the bones of both my shins but thankfully I never needed to be in plaster!

On the wild winter walk described above, we were unprepared. We had served very sparse apprenticeships and we were out there primarily for fun. We were out of our depth in an unfamiliar environment and the injuries sustained could easily have been avoided. We had fun and have great memories of an exciting weekend in the wilds of Scotland, but we were walking a very fine line between adventure and emergency, between sense and stupidity, even between life and death. Adventure can be most enjoyed when prepared for. We had not prepared at all. We were unlike the wild young adventurer David. Standing alone on a battlefield against a giant, who was championed as a killer of many warriors, is more dangerous than any winter walk. David, though, had served an apprenticeship as we see in his response to Saul's questioning his readiness to face Goliath. David reminds Saul that - "When a lion or a bear came and carried off a sheep from the flock, I went after it, struck it and rescued the sheep from its mouth. When it turned on me, I seized it by its hair, struck it and killed it. Your servant has killed both the lion and the bear; this Philistine will be like one of them for he has defied the armies of the living God" (1 Samuel 17:34-36). David shows that he was prepared, he had lived a life of adventure and through it had learned how to face risk and conquer.

David also showed that he did not fight bears and lions and walk out to face Goliath for the sake of danger alone. He was no adrenaline junkie going out to fight a giant for a quick fix. He was aware that Goliath and the Philistine armies were in the wrong, they had "defied the armies of the living God" and for that reason he had been called to act. David went on to show an awareness that it was not by his own strength that he overcame his aggressors, and that it was not by his own strength that he walked out to face the giant. He states "The Lord who delivered me from the paw of the lion and the paw of the bear will deliver me from the hand of this Philistine" (1 Samuel 17:37). And in the final preparations for confrontation we read that David did not take chances. He knew God was calling him to do this, and he responded by doing it to the very best of his ability. That included preparing as fully as possible. We read that David "took his staff in his hand, chose five smooth stones from the stream, put them in the pouch of his shepherd's bag and, with his sling in his hand, approached the Philistine" (1 Samuel 17:40). David did not pick up any old stone on the way to the battle. He chose stones that would be most effective, ones that had been smoothed off and shaped by the flow of the river. And he did not just pick up one and set off with that. It was with the first stone the giant was felled, but David had another four in his bag just in case. He was ready to do the will of God to the very best of his ability.

When in the hills with some close friends on a recent outing, we spent an afternoon alone. This time was spent wandering around exploring, sitting and meditating, and praising and worshipping the God who created the surroundings. During this time, one of my friends headed high up the mountainside at the foot of which we were based. He came back hours later, covered in mud and grass. Sweating and still out of breath from his adventurous journey, the most noticeable thing though was the light in his eyes, for he had gone out and faced a challenge. He had conquered, and through it had grown closer to God. Knowledge gained through years of bible study had almost instantly moved from his head to his heart, and in the same moment he became more fully alive than ever. While high above the valley floor he had taken some pictures, including one of himself. Weeks later, his wife commented that in that picture there was a spark in her husband's eyes she hadn't seen for a long time. In that picture he was an adventurer, exploring God in His wild creation. If that mindset - that intense feeling of taking life by the reigns and going for it no matter what the risk - if that can be applied to all of life, then we can change the world. It is a choice. Just like walking in the wilds is a choice. We can choose to live a life of adventure.

Everyone can benefit from facing the risks using the common sense we have been created with, rather than paying to read about or watch other peoples' experiences. Imagine if our biblical heroes had risk assessed everything. Do you think David would have gone out and faced Goliath wearing no armour? Should Peter have tried walking on water with no life jacket? And what about the adventures of Paul? Would he have even ventured onto ships with no low-level safety lighting, emergency exits or life rafts? Many safety features make sense of course, but safety consciousness and risk avoidance has gone much too far in many areas already. The impact is that many Christians no longer live a life of adventure like our biblical heroes. Too many people now focus so much on the here and now that an eternal perspective is an alien concept. The focus is almost entirely on preserving life, on saving for a rainy day, on preparing for the latter years of this short life. Comforts, quick fixes and safety consciousness rule the day. Ironically, as the focus is on physical safety and comfort, our spiritual life is pushed further into the realms of danger. Many of the courageous attitudes that come through knowing that we have already stepped into life eternal have been lost. Now despite no risk of losing our heads for our faith, we worry about speaking the name of Jesus in case we lose face. With no risk of being burnt at the stake, we now worry about a few 'singeing' jokes!

We can all live fully in the adventure of life with Christ. Jesus is the ultimate hero ever to have walked the earth. We can arise from our slumber and be like Him. Right at the start of Jesus' three-year ministry he went out alone on the wildest of adventures. He was born into an adventure of course, but before he started the final three years of His time on earth - three years that would change the world - He had a wild adventure. Jesus went off into the desert wilderness, fasting and preparing for what was to come, and out there alone in the wild he came face-to-face with His enemy. Alone He stood firm and let the enemy know who He was. Afterwards He returned to society and changed the world.

We can overcome the hazard of a risk free life. We can, like every hero who has gone before us, die to self, knowing more fully the truth that declares 'to live is Christ and to die is gain' (Philippians 1:21). We can see the insignificance of the risk involved in getting to a wild place to kneel before our Father, when we know that as a result we can live a life that is a purpose driven adventure, a life of blessing and fulfilment. The whole of life can be a wild adventure. Let's not be blinkered by the world's obsession with safety and comfort!

Loose scree slopes on which every rock moves and grinds against those below and beside. Where every footstep causes the ground to move and the whole slope feels as though it could release its grip and roll toward the flatland far below. Through knee-deep heather that hides obstacles beneath its purple bloom and scratchy stems. Rabbit-holes that may turn my ankle. Boulders that might jar my knee. Along leaf-strewn trails where half-hidden roots cause my feet to slip and where the dampness negates all grip. Under woodland canopies that sway in gales that blow. Great trunks and limbs moved by the force threaten to join those previously blown over, that now lie, moss-covered, all around. In open places I could wander in circles, lost, as the mist moves in and suddenly all directions blend into one under a continuous cloak of grey. When cloud comes down and touches snow I might feel like a tiny two-dimensional figure lost in a vast blank canvas. A place where only whiteness exists, where there is no distinction between earth and sky and where perception of distance and direction is distorted. When the rain pours down and floodwaters rise and every footstep taken is as tentative as those of Peter on the waters surface, still, in all these places I will determinedly follow.

No matter how hard the conditions and no matter what risk the journey entails, still I will follow. No matter how uneven the ground, invisible the direction or unpredictable the weather, still I will follow. I will follow in the footsteps of the One who risked it all for me. Jesus died for me. I will follow only Him. This rocky height where the rocks move underfoot, this is my Mount Hermon, the place where I meet my Father and welcome His transforming power. And as I move from rocky heights to lower hills among the Pine and Birch, now this is my Mount of Olives. I am here to kneel before my God, to seek His intimate presence. From the small wooded hills to the shore-line with cold loch water lapping and tree roots stretching out over slippery rocks to drink, this is my sea of Galilee. Here all distractions are removed. No crowds. No busyness. Just my Father, His beautiful creation and me. On this woodland path leading up and away from the loch, this is my hillside near Galilee; this is where I come to taste living water and to have my hunger satisfied. In these wild landscapes, through woodlands and along loch-sides, from sea to summit I will walk. I will follow footprints with each step I take. I follow in the footsteps of Jesus Christ. It is thanks to Him that I can be here in the courts of my Father, enjoying His presence, and revelling in the blessing of this life of adventure with Him. Risk? Risk has never seemed so irrelevant.

A Few Words of Caution

Nature as an end in itself, is empty.

See, Hear, Smell, Taste, Feel... Know

Have you ever tasted pure cold water straight from a burn? Have you lain back on sun-warmed rock and felt heat rise through your body? Have you smelt sweet tree sap on a warm day, or the fresh scent of the forest immediately after the rain has fallen? Have you tasted the tangy little Wood Sorrel, or berries picked straight from the briar? What about the sweetness of wild strawberries? Have you listened to the vast array of birdsong that fills the forest or the long haunting cry of the buzzard or eagle? Have you listened to the sound of a stag's call filling a remote valley? Have you felt the spray from a waterfall as it settles upon your face? Have you felt the power of flowing water when you have plunged your hand into a stream? Have you listened, as its roar has become only a gentle babble further up the valley? Have you felt the crispness of an autumn leaf plucked straight from the air as it fell toward the forest floor? Have you heard the rustle as you walk over the newly-laid carpet of browns and reds and gold? Or what of the snow? Have you felt it judder under foot as your weight compresses flakes together? Have you heard its muffled sound as you lay fresh *tracks on frozen surface? Have you smelt the fresh fragrance of spring flowers as they burst forth from dark earth? Have you walked and let your fingers trail through tall meadow grasses? Have you heard the seedpods on the broom plant pop as the warm sunlight triggers them to burst? Have you heard the faint patter of their scattered seed? Have you smelt the coconut-scented gorse as its yellow flowers reach full bloom? Have you lain down in wild meadows and drifted in and out of sleep, the smells of summer filling you with each inhalation, and birdsong, the breeze rustled leaves, the wind in the grass, the trickle of the burn - such sounds of nature in your ears? Such a wonderful wild creation and that doesn't even touch on what you can see!*

 When we look at an object, we instantly see it as it is. Seeing is something we usually take for granted, yet sight requires an incredibly complex process involving the transfer and processing of vast amounts of information at a phenomenal rate. An image, illuminated by light, is transferred via the lens of the eye and projected, upside down, onto the retina where light receptors are contained. Despite the fact that we capture the image upside down, the processing of it happens so fast that we look around and see things almost instantaneously the right way up!

Think about these words you are reading. Each character is captured upside down on your retina and instantly processed for depth, form, colour, and motion – or lack thereof. Add to this processing the application of knowledge, and suddenly you see each character in the context of a word. Each word is linked to the word before and after and the sentence is understood. Each sentence is understood in the context of the paragraph, the chapter, the book, and is linked to all the existing information already held in the vastness of the brain. Without looking around now, you know where you are. You can partly see it in your peripheral vision, but also, before you sat down you will have sub-consciously captured and processed the whole scene and stored it in your memory so that you are aware of your place in physical space! On top of all this is the diverse and complex range of emotions and feelings and other factors that are applied to what you see, and are triggered by it! The fact that we can see is mind-blowing to say the least.

We have sight; let's appreciate it and use it to get to know God more. Let's take time to look around at what God has made! We need to stop and appreciate it in the context of our faith. Stopping and looking at the finer details, appreciating what has been made, and pondering what is revealed through it shifts our view from that of worldly perspective to that of spiritual perspective.

Taste has not always been considered a sense in its own right. Due to food coming into direct contact with the tongue, (an organ predominantly consisting of a number of complex muscles), taste has, in the past, been considered to be a form of touch. Now however, knowledge of the human body and its functions has expanded and taste is not only recognised as a sense in its own right, but is catered for extensively. Just think of the vast array of products available on the shelves of supermarkets. A whole industry has been built up on the strength of this single sense!

Specific areas of our tongue are dedicated to four different tastes. Sweet is at the tip of the tongue, bitter is farther back and salt and sour are located at different points along the edges. Just four divisions, yet our tongues are capable of picking out the subtle differences. For example, there are those who can taste wine and distinguish not only the grape type, but also the region where the grape was grown. Some can even tell the year it was produced! Food specialists can distinguish between numerous ingredients in a single dish, and know how to alter the quantities of each in order to bring out the best in the food. Lindsay and I have a good friend who can tell what part of Scotland a Salmon lived in before it was caught, smoked, and served up for her to taste!

Our attitudes to taste and eating are almost a parallel to our changing attitudes to life as a whole in this era of convenience. The closest many of us now get to digging for vegetables is when we plunge our hands into the deep freezer at the supermarket and pull out the ready cleaned, chopped and packaged parsnips, potatoes, carrots, peas or any other conveniently processed vegetable! Convenience has become a major selling point. From microwave meals to ready washed and chopped salads and pre grated cheese, the speed and ease with which food can be prepared is promoted as the very reason for buying it. Yet through this speed and ease we do not seem to have much more time for enjoying some stillness in our lives. Often it seems that we simply use the extra time to cram more in. Sitting at the table for a family meal is, for too many people, a thing of the past. Many people now eat at different times, often just grab a convenience meal and pop it in the microwave, eat while watching a bit of television, swallow a couple of antacids for pudding then its back to their busy schedule! We need to slow it all down and to recognise the importance of stillness in our lives. We need to allow our senses time to really enjoy what we have.

Going slow and being still are aspects of living that are vital to a healthy relationship with God, yet they are aspects that are becoming increasingly alien to many people. We need to battle against the tides and trends of the speed obsessed world around us and engage in some time lying in 'green pastures' and time wandering beside 'still waters'. Through such sensory stimulation our soul can be restored and we can live more as God intended.

Outdoors, being still, gives us opportunity to see more of the diversity and smaller details of creation. Too often when moving around, particularly on rougher ground, our eyes remain fixed to the trail, focused intently upon each new foot placement so that the wonders of the natural scene around us are all but invisible. And we are not exactly creatures of stealth! Twigs snapping underfoot, clothing rustling, stones crunching with each step, breathing loudly due to the required effort. No wonder wildlife runs for cover! Stop though, sit and be still, and in the silence the world around comes alive with creatures that would otherwise have gone unnoticed. I have sat still and watched a woodpecker drill into an old tree stump. I have watched a badger emerge from its burrow in the half-light of dusk, and make its way along a well-worn path at the side of the river. I have lain in the heather and watched a stag throw back its antlers and call out across the valley. I would not have enjoyed seeing any of these if I had been moving. And when we are still and silent we can hear more around us as well.

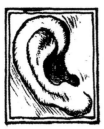

It is not only sound that the ear is responsible for. Sensing gravity and enhancing balance are also the functions of those strangely shaped things on the sides of your head! Sound itself is energy transfer, the movement of air caused by the motion or vibration of an object. Still air consists of molecules of nitrogen, oxygen and carbon dioxide. Despite the air being 'still', these molecules are in constant random motion. A movement or vibration causes these molecules to be pushed in a certain way. They bang into other molecules, which in turn bang into others and so on, so that through such a chain reaction sound can travel at incredible speed.

When moving particles reach the ear, a near miraculous process begins that captures these moving particles and transforms them into vibrations which are then transferred to the brain where they are recognised as a specific sound. The outer ears function is to capture the moving air and funnel it toward the eardrum, which vibrates in response. This is the similar effect that an empty shell can have, where low level noise is funnelled into the cavernous inner shell where it ricochets off the walls until its energy is depleted. The shell captures the noise of the sea, or the low level noise in any situation. With the shell pressed to our ear we hear the captured sound as waves. The shell directs our mind toward the sea, just as the sounds, sights, smells, tastes, and textures of the natural world direct our minds toward their creator. Amazingly when our outer ear functions, it not only captures the sound, but allows us to discern the direction from which it emanates, or even the specific object that has caused it.

The airtight cavity of the middle ear forms a protective seal and through this the three smallest bones of the body (the malleus, incus and stapes) are linked in a way that enables the vibrations to be transferred through the seal and into the inner ear. These vibrations of the ear are minute. The movements of the basilar membrane, for example, have been measured at 10 – 100 nanometres. A nanometre is a millionth of a millimetre!

It is incredible to think of the work being carried out by the ear when we consider the noisy bustling world we live in. Think of a city and the chaos of noise that the ear and brain must capture and decipher in order to make sense of what we hear. Horns, engines, shouting, music, tyres on tarmac, brakes squealing, children squealing, parents shouting, doors banging, airplanes over head, dogs barking, alarms ringing, sirens blaring, all differentiated and transferred to the brain through the tiniest of vibrations. No wonder silence is soothing to the ear!

The ears of a fox are more sensitive than those of the human, yet through being still, Lindsay enjoyed a close encounter with a little red-coated fox. She had been out on one of her weekly wanders, along the top edge of a little wooded ravine. It was a misty drizzly day, grey clouds overhead and water dripping from every branch. Lindsay had stopped and stood beside an old Oak tree, cup of tea in hand, enjoying a time of stillness in a busy week. The fox came wandering along the track and stopped within a few metres of her. There it stood, looking out across the harvested fields, while Lindsay stood watching it. It looked round and for a couple of seconds they stared at each other before the fox darted away.

I wonder had the fox got used to having the trail to itself when the weather was grey and wet? The weather does seem to put a lot of people off going outdoors. Yet getting out in all weather allows us to enjoy God's creation in even more ways. There is something enjoyable about walking in the rain, sheltering under trees listening to the sounds of rain on the canopy above. Smelling the newly wetted ground. Seeing leaves glisten and drips of water hang on every tip. In the wind too, a normally still scene can be transformed to one of movement, as trees sway and creak, leaves blow, and birds dart for cover. With the snow comes the most dramatic transformation, when the whole world turns white and silent. Branches and treetops bend under the weight of snow, light fills every corner of creation, bouncing off the new white cover at every conceivable angle. Every weather condition has its own merit, its own particular beauty, and its own effect upon the mind and spirit. Yet it is often what we *feel* that puts us off going out when the weather is cold or wet.

 As senses go, touch is very different to the other four. The organs enabling sight, hearing, smell and taste are all located in the head. Touch, however, is enabled by the numerous nerve endings that link our brain to just under the pigment-bearing layer (the malphigian layer) of our skin. Beyond the malphigian layer is the epidermis, and the outer layer of this is basically a covering of dead tissue that is constantly wearing away and being replaced from below. The nerves are so sensitive, and positioned so close to this dead layer that we are capable of very sensitive feeling. A single raindrop can be felt almost anywhere on the body that we allow it to land on! Elbows are an exception. Straighten your arm, and then using your other hand, pinch the area of loose skin at what would normally be the outer bend of your elbow. Go on, squeeze, you will feel no pain!

Like seeing, hearing, tasting and smelling, feeling seems instantaneous, but it involves rapid information transfer and processing. The sensation of pain can reveal the fraction of time this process takes. Lifting something that is too hot for example, can take time to register and for the message to return from your brain to the fingers so they release their grip. Think about it next time you are standing with your hand under the cold, running water!

This sense of touch means that we know when to withdraw and protect ourselves, when to seek heat or shade, and even when we need to rest our bodies. As well as self-preservation, feeling enables pleasure. The feeling of a cool breeze on a hot day, or heat on a cold one. A warm bath when muscles ache. A hand placed on the grain of ancient rock. The feeling of sponge like moss. The feeling of a fish on the end of the line. Soft grass forming a bed beneath us. Warm sunrays upon us. Rain splashing down on us when we know we will soon be dry and warm. Have you felt the wild creation that surrounds you? Have you felt it, and known more of its creator?

The nose protrudes from the centre of each human face in a vast array of shapes and sizes! The part concerned with smell however, is no bigger than the size of two postage stamps and is situated at the top of the nose, underneath the bridge. During normal breathing air passes through he nose at a rate of some 250 millilitres per second and only a little of that passes over the postage stamp sized olfactory bulb. With a sniff, the air intake can be quadrupled and it travels higher into the nasal cavity, fully immersing the olfactory bulb in whatever scents the air is carrying. Under a powerful microscope the olfactory bulb looks like a plate of spaghetti. Each strand of 'spaghetti' protrudes from a receptor cell and in each and every human being there can be upward of 10 million receptor cells. At the end of each strand of 'spaghetti' there are five olfactory hairs. That is approximately 50 million scent sensing hairs in any one human, and all contained in an area no bigger than two postage stamps! Even more fascinating is the fact that these hairs are actually outward protrusions of the brain! It is hardly surprising therefore that scent can trigger such powerful memories and emotions. French novelist Marcel Proust had such a flood of emotions stirred by the smell of tea and toast, that he based most of his literary work upon it!

God has created us with five senses; we should apply them all when we go out into His creation. We can enjoy the feeling of being fully alive when we stop taking our senses for granted and allow them to be stimulated. In a way it can make us feel more human - more real - for in appreciating our senses we appreciate who we are. From every sense information floods rapidly toward our brain and clears away the sluggishness that we get too accustomed to.

It is the flood of sensation that can wake us fully, the flood of information that the senses send to the brain that raises the hairs on our necks; that causes a shiver; that triggers something deeper; that stirs those deep places and can alert us to the presence of God in our lives. Every one of our senses can evoke feeling and direct our mind to God. Every one of our senses can be stimulated by what our great creator God has made. Through seeing, hearing, feeling, tasting and smelling the world around us we can know more of our awesome loving God.

It's that faint smell, carried on the most gentle of breezes. That's what it is. That faint smell that triggers this strong memory. More than memory, perhaps more like longing. I do not know where or from what it emanates. Maybe those Pines far down the valley, or the river. Maybe it comes from the earth itself. That covering of life-sustaining earth spread so thinly across the bedrock of this landscape. The scent itself is indescribable in its delicacy. At times it seems to disappear, then at the end of an inhalation or even the point between inhale and exhale, it is there again for the briefest of moments, then is lost again as lungs inflate or deflate. The feeling, the emotion, remains. How can something so barely perceptible and indescribable evoke such strong emotion? Like the smell of cut grass and the memories it conjures in the mind. Memories of the long warm summer days of childhood. Maybe the smell of cut grass evokes more than memory; maybe it is like this delicate aroma on the hillside.

Maybe there is a sense of longing evoked too. Longing for the happiness, innocence, laughter, and freedom, that is associated with those halcyon days. Days when there is no pain or tiredness, an escape from weariness, and a longing for home. Yes, that is what I am feeling. This faint aroma has evoked a longing for my home in heaven and all the deep joys that await me there.

THE FREEDOM CHAPTERS

Layers

Imagine a whole nation that is densely covered with trees. The people of this imaginary nation spend their lives busily working, playing, and relaxing - living their entire lives between the trunks, in a place where sunlight is filtered through the thick leafy canopy above. Occasionally someone sees a glimmer of light that reaches the forest floor. This light kindles a desire within those who see it; it is a desire to know more of what lies above the trunks, a desire to focus on what is beyond what they usually see. They long for more, they long to see more, feel more, and know more. So up they go. Up they go until suddenly they can push their faces through the canopy of green and what a wonderful experience it is. Suddenly they know that a vast world of blue sky and pure light rises above and dwarfs that which was previously seen as their complete world. Their world now has a new context. They know that a powerful light above causes the canopy to grow, and become green, and facilitates life below. When they climb back down they have a whole new perspective. They see the world between the trunks differently. They have experienced a paradigm shift.

> "Do not conform any longer to the pattern of this world, but be transformed by the renewing of your mind. Then you will be able to test and approve what God's will is - his good, pleasing and perfect will." (Romans 12:2)

In our world there are many layers. There is the layer of physical creation: that which God spoke into being before He made mankind. That which God created by saying the words, 'Let there be light... Let there be an expanse between the waters... Let the water under the sky be gathered into one place... Let dry ground appear... Let the land produce vegetation... Let there be lights in the sky... Let the waters teem with living creatures and let birds fly above the earth across the expanse of sky... Let the land produce living creatures' (Genesis 1:1-24, selected verses).

After six days there it was - the physical landscape - new and wonderful, bringing glory to its creator. The landscape of creation, perfect, and beautiful beyond description. But God had not finished and in that paradise He created and placed man. He made man in His own image and set him apart from the rest of creation, ordaining that man should 'rule over the fish of the sea and the birds of the air, over the livestock, over all the earth and over all the creatures that move along the ground' (Genesis 1:26). God also tells man to 'be fruitful and increase in number; fill the earth and subdue it' (Genesis 1:28). So onto the layer of physical creation God places the social layer of mankind. A layer separate and distinct from the wild landscape, yet at the same time inherently linked to it. Intrinsically linked to it because of man's relationship with God. Man is given the role of caring for the physical creation with which God is pleased.

God eternal, the first 'layer', is there before all else, there with no beginning and no end, and by whom the new layers are created. The layer of physical creation: the sun, moon, earth, the soil and all plant and animal life. And the layer of society with man given responsibility for much of the physical landscape. Man, created in the image of the creator. He is even given the gift of free will and it does not take long before he uses it to turn His back on God.

Suddenly there is separation between the layers. God no longer walks with man through the garden. In fact, man is cast out of the garden and now faces death. God however loves man so much that he sends His only son to earth to pay our debt and make reconciliation and life possible. Jesus rose again and now God can dwell within us through the Holy Spirit when we acknowledge Jesus as our Saviour and give our lives to Him. With our free will we each have the opportunity to either accept or reject this truth. There is no in-between. Now much of the society around us reveals man doing his own thing. It is a world of good and evil. A battle between these two sides continues. Rather than ruling over the earth in a caring way as ordained at the point of creation, mankind now largely exploits and destroys it. Much of mankind has turned its back on the spiritual realm and also on the physical landscape of wild creation. Man once walked with God in the Garden of Eden, and because of Jesus we can walk with God again. But with whole lives being lived out in the townscapes and cityscapes of the social layer we are part of a social world more separate than ever from the loving creator God. It is like that imaginary tree-covered nation, but instead of tree trunks it is one of buildings and streets, concrete and tarmac, straight lines and flat surfaces. Hiding the supernatural realm is a canopy of self-obsession, self-indulgence, self-fulfilment, self, self, self.

We need to find a space where we can see even more of what really surrounds us, where the supernatural realm is clearly revealed. We need to spend time in the physical landscape for when we do, it is as though we push our faces through the thick canopy. We see the heavens that declare God's glory, skies that proclaim the work of His hands. We see a whole wild creation that reveals the divine and eternal nature of our God. We need this place, free of all the mixed up ideas of a society that no longer sees its Creator, that has lost its history and that searches desperately for any other explanation as to where we have come from, why we are here and where we are going. When we accept the truth, when we see that glimmer of light piercing through the canopy, we need to follow it. It is for freedom that Christ has set us free. It is freedom we should fully enjoy.

As We Have Been Created
(Freedom from Identity Crises)

One of the seals turns itself awkwardly and shuffles clumsily and laboriously, toward the water. The other two lie motionless. Into the water it slips and instantly the lump of blubber becomes a most elegant and graceful shadow darting through the water, turning this way and that. It rises and pushes its head above the surface then without a sound and barely a ripple plunges downward, almost vertically, and disappears into the cold depths below. Now it reappears, at the surface, close to the boat, and peers at everyone on board. There it hangs in the water, weightless. This animal is not made for land; it is created perfectly for life among the waves. It knows where it is most at home, and there it dances through the water. Beauty in motion. Doing what it is created to do and doing it beautifully.

A bird balances on the rail of the boat. Its brown feathers ruffle in the wind as it struggles not to fall off. The rocking of the boat and the buffeting wind have it wobbling and jerking its wings to stay on board. With awkward little side-steps and hops, it edges along the railing. Its head turns towards the sea, jet black eyes looking out over the churning waves.

Its powerful hooked beak gives it a determined look. Then its wings are spread and without a sound it soars up and away into the grey skies. It arcs and turns, using the wind. Gliding, swooping, rising. Graceful flight. This bird is made to fly. It is made for the air.

Who are you?

How often when we are asked that question do we describe what we do? The job we do or the careers we have, the past-times we enjoy, our family, who we know, where we come from, what sport we follow, what team we support, or anything else we fill our time with is offered in answer to the question of who we are. "I am a... I'm interested in... I come from... I work as... I live in... My wife is... My husband is... My children are... I own a... My house is... I drive a..." Anything we do, or have, that gives us a sense of identity is seen as a valid way of describing who we are. But is that really who you are? No? Then who are you? Who is the real you? What is it that separates you from every other person on the face of the earth? What is left of you when everything else is stripped away?

In the past when asked who I was, I would have been delighted with the opportunity to talk about my exploits on bicycles for as long as anyone would listen! I was a cyclist - a Lycra-clad, shaven-legged, training, racing, competitive, ambitious cyclist. I was striving to make it to the top in this chosen sport. The professionals in the glossy magazines were my heroes; I wanted to be like them. Cycling shaped me: what I wore, what I read, where I went and whom I spent time with were all aspects of my life that were influenced by the sport. It even shaped my body. My legs looked like cycling legs with cuts and scrapes and scars, and my heart was also affected. When I was resting it would beat around 45 times a minute. When I was racing up a hill it could reach as high as 190. I was a cyclist, or so I thought. The real me, the individual created in God's likeness, lay buried under a pile of race results, ambitions, and expensive bicycles.

Sometimes it seems that our real self lies so buried that we do not even really know who we are, as we twist and turn and change with every new idea, every new person we meet, every trend and fad. We start to see ourselves first and foremost in relation to the thing we pursue or what we do. It's like chasing an illusion, one that when understood in light of the bigger picture seems utterly shallow. When that thing that gives us a temporary identity is gone, with it goes any associated sense of purpose and certainty. Who are we then? Does our introduction then start with 'I was...' or 'I could have been...' or 'I had...'? Do we lose some of our identity because we have relied upon things that pass away even faster than we do?

So many people seem to make it to the end of the dream they were chasing, only to find emptiness. The illusion is recognised as just that, a cheap trick that offers none of what really inspires, amazes, and satisfies. The illusion starts out as something appealing and attractive, something that calls out to that deeper longing within us. Through chasing it we lose sight of who we are. We get dulled and buried by a whole concoction of things that have wrongly become our goal - or even our idol. We conform to the pattern of the world when we should be 'set apart', 'aliens', in this world, but often we are as far from fitting that description as the peak of Everest is from the depths of the deepest sea.

During the years my life was based around cycling, I was distant from God. I had long before then made a commitment, but I had allowed myself to continue living with a short-term perspective. My long-term thinking went little further than the next racing season. I worshipped the Lycra-clad professionals in the magazines, and my praise was reserved for the latest bike that cost so much it was frightening to ride. I know I am not the only one who has given their life to God and then continued to live wearing the masks of past identities. We give our lives to God but continue to live in a world that has little time for contemplation of that which is beyond the realm we see around us. Paul tells us in a letter to the Corinthians that we should not be tied down to this realm like the rest of the world, but as believers we should live a life set apart from the empty ways of the world (2 Corinthians 6:17). I had failed at this.

Wild places offer physical separation from society of course, but to be beneficial they need to be approached in the right way. I did spend time in wild places during this cycling period, but those places swept past the edge of my sight in a sweat filled blur as I pushed myself, feeling sick and with lungs burning, up another hill. Then I would speed down and start all over again. I approached wild places as a training ground. I went to wild places as a cyclist. I didn't have time to stop and ponder what was around me; I was there mainly to train. I didn't have time to sit and pray and meet with God because there always seemed to be a race quickly approaching. Rather than finding out what God had planned for my life from the very beginning, I was too busy dreaming of being a champion in this world, of being seen by those around me as a success. And I know that I am far from alone in spending too much time and effort living for the here and now. I have seen many fellow believers in the same boat, and the consequences are always to the detriment of our relationship with God.

A pile of stones marks the highest spot on this little hill. A simple cross rises from it. Two thin branches bound together with an old piece of rope. The ends of the rope swing gently in the warm breeze. Such simplicity representing such complexity. Love unfathomable leading to death. Death overcome, leading to life. Life for me; life for all - life eternal. That is what is really important. That reward far outweighs any medal. The victory of Jesus on the cross is now the only win that I will boast of.

Each and every one of us is created for a reason. We are no accident. I know that I am much more than a cyclist. I just needed to take time away from it all and seek God and His plan for my life. I needed to take time and ask forgiveness for putting so many things before God, and to ask Him to show me who I was and what I was here for. We all need to take time, away from worldly attractions. We need to bring ourselves before God. We need to do what Jesus did. We need to walk into quiet corners of wild creation and get on our knees. Get on our knees among the purple summer heather, among fallen autumn leaves, on the soft white snow, among the flowers and grasses of the meadows, by a meandering burn, on a wind swept summit. We need to open ourselves to being led by God near quiet waters, to being made to lie down in green pastures, to having our souls fully restored. We need to take our eyes off ourselves and meet with God intimately, with no time restrictions and with no distractions. We need to come out and be separate from the world. Be different, and real, and become who we have been created to be from the very beginning.

There is a process, referred to by psychologists as 'Interpolation'. It is a process that describes how we are fed dreams and ambitions. Advertising works through this process, and is responsible for much of it, though it is apparent in many areas of life. Imagine walking down the street: you are not hungry, you are just the right temperature, feeling well, and needing nothing. Then you see an advertisement board, depicting some new attractive product. Suddenly you think, "If only I had that, if only I was like that, if only I could do that, then I would be complete, then other people would know and see who I am. I would be significant. I would be more successful". In an instant we can go from being happy and content to being restless, distracted and striving after something. It may have called to a deeper part of us that longs for purpose, but unless it is of God then it is just another fleeting thing that has the potential to distract us from the only place we can find true satisfaction. Even when we do need some of the basics such as food, water, or shelter, our satisfaction can still only really come from our Father.

We can see elements of this interpolation process used by Satan to tempt Jesus in the desert. Starting at Matthew 3:2, the scene is set with a great understatement! "After fasting for forty days and nights, he (Jesus) was hungry." Satan begins by appealing to Jesus' physical desire, "If you are the Son of God, tell these stones to become bread" (verse 3). As well as appealing to His hunger, Satan is suggesting that Jesus needs to validate His claim that He is the Son of God. Jesus however is not only confident in the knowledge of who he is, but also uses scripture to repel the food temptation, "It is written: ' Man cannot live on bread alone, but on every word that comes from the mouth of God" (verse 4). Reading on we find that Satan leads Jesus to the top of the temple roof and again tries to appeal to pride, asking Jesus to validate himself by jumping from the roof. What Satan is saying is, 'I don't believe you are who you say you are so prove it.' Satan cunningly uses something of utmost importance to make this more tempting - Holy Scripture - but he takes it out of context, "If you are the Son of God throw yourself down. For it is written: 'He will command his angels concerning you, and they will lift you up in their hands, so that you will not strike your foot against a stone'" (verse 6). Again Jesus is absolutely secure in His identity, so that it does not matter whether Satan believes Him or not. Jesus again resists temptation, and again uses scripture in response, "Jesus answered him, 'It is also written: 'Do not put the Lord your God to the test'" (verse 7). For the final temptation Jesus is taken to "a very high mountain" and from there Satan shows Him every kingdom of the world with all their riches and splendour. After viewing all the kingdoms Satan states that "All this I will give to you if you will bow down and worship me" (verse 9). You can see what he is saying here: if you have all this you will be significant, all these riches will be yours and surely that will make you happy, this is who you could be, you could be ruler over all this. Satan thinks he can appeal to deep desires in Jesus' heart by flashing before Him all the amazing riches and the chance for Jesus to be ruler over all. However, Jesus remains focused on His true self, in relation to His Father. He is not tempted to take on some false identity because all the kingdoms have been presented before Him. 'Jesus said to him, "Away from me Satan! For it is written: 'Worship the Lord your God, and serve him only'" (verse 10). Satan was acting like an advertisement board, trying to lure Jesus away from where He was really headed, trying to sell Him another dream that would distract Him from the true course laid out before Him. Jesus had spent forty days, alone with His Father amidst some of the wildest natural terrain. Jesus knew who He was, why He was here on earth and what He had been called to do.

Because Jesus remained focused He has gone down in history as the greatest hero there has ever been and He is the greatest hero there ever will be. Jesus Christ, the Son of God gave His life freely so that we can live. Because of Jesus we can be born again into a life that will never end. We can be saved because Jesus died for us. What incredible words of truth. Yet with time and through familiarity, and with hearing or reading these words again and again it seems their impact can be reduced. These words of truth can blow over us like a breeze against a mountain, their power barely felt. Yet they are words that should hit us like a gale against a forest. When a gale blasts against the trees any dead branches are knocked to the ground as the whole forest sways under the force. Similarly those words should leave us feeling fresh, shaken, restored, and renewed every time. The problem is that, until we turn to God, we have a sinful nature and we live in a world where short term and empty things are valued. We need to remain focused on who we really are and resist all the other identities so readily on offer.

Mountains rise on every side. Gullies, pinnacles, peaks and valleys highlighted by shadows cast in the early-morning light. The pool-side terrace is one of the best places to view these giants as sunlight flows slowly down their flanks until it floods the inhabited valleys below. All around their peaks rise into another days clear-blue sky.

So much surrounding grandeur and yet it is to the poolside my gaze is drawn. There sits the little toad in the morning light. There he sits poised, ready to hop. He is not the dark-green of his warty Scottish relations but more of a creamy-green flecked with brown, like the camouflage uniforms worn by soldiers for desert combat. I guess their purpose is similar.

He must have left his mountain stream during the night and made his way over the cool dewy grass to find himself here by the pool. His big round, black and bulging eyes stare out of a face that seems to have a grin spread permanently across it. I wonder what he thinks. I wonder does he weigh up his mountain stream against this clear fresh looking blue water of the swimming pool? As the first rays of sunlight reach his little cool damp loving body, does he consider that the hop into the clear blue is a better option than the journey back to the stream through rapidly drying grass and earth? The pool is something new. Something that must look bigger, fresher, clearer, more appealing than the place he has just left.

Decision made, he hops and with a smooth, near splashless dive, he has gone from above to below. Small circular ripples spread out wider and wider as down and down he swims. At first it must feel so good. Paradise, he must think, has been found. Paradise that he is swimming down through, relishing the feel of the cool water on his previously dry dusty skin. I watch his strong back legs as they kick out and thrust him downwards. The webbing between his toes act like powerful flippers. His small front legs are folded neatly along his sides as he plunges deeper, headfirst, streamlined, through the water. Down and down until he reaches the bottom, where he finds there is nothing to grip. He needs something to hold onto. Without it his little air-filled lungs act like a buoyancy aid and soon have him bobbing back on the surface.

His tiring legs start to slow, no longer kicking powerfully together. Now it is one then the other, peddling at the water. The front arms are now stretched out before him scrabbling desperately for something to hold. What had seemed like paradise is found to be empty. His legs stop kicking and he floats gently to the surface.

His head pops through the surface first. Legs, now still, stretch out behind him. In the pump-circulated pool water he spins in pointless circles. His black eyes continue to stare as he turns with the surface water. Is that confusion amidst their inky blackness? Down and down he plunges again, searching the bottom, searching along the edges, searching for anything to grasp. All he finds again is the same blue emptiness, and bodies. Bodies of dead insects. Is it now he notices the chemicals? For it is chemicals and pumps and filters that keep the water clear, keep it looking good. It doesn't pour over rocks, naturally oxygenated by its cascading flow. It is not naturally filtered through stone and sand. Is that desperation now in his clutching front legs? He bobs to the surface again. Is that fear now that glints in his little black eyes?

He swims toward the side, but there is no escape. Frantically his front legs scrabble at the smooth sides while his back legs kick uselessly at the water. He is trapped. Now he is still, except for his pulsating throat, that moves rapidly with the filling of his little lungs or pounding heart. Floating again in pointless circles, little ripples spread out in arcs from his throat. Their reflection can be seen as faint waves of light moving along the smooth pool bottom then fading away, like the illusion this blue paradise turned out to be.

I reach down and place my hand gently into the water in front of the little toad. Surprisingly he shows no hesitation and gladly accepts the lift back to solid ground. Off he goes without looking back. He hops away toward the familiar mountain stream.

We have to choose. Do we accept the identity we were originally created to have - the real us that brings glory to God - or do we continue shuffling along living a veiled life, switching from one temporary mask to another? Do we focus on the long term and remain in the place we are meant to be, or do we chase after any short-term thing that glitters and appears to offer some immediate reward? If we fail to focus on the real life stretching out before us, and jump into any new thing that comes our way, we are like the little toad who runs the risk of swimming about in a world of emptiness where there is nothing solid to grasp. Only God offers that long-term hope and reality.

God's grace that was extended to us and the sacrifice

Jesus made, the ultimate act of love, should be at the very core of who we are. Jesus Christ, the Son of the Living God, wholly innocent, perfect in every way stood before those He came to save and was judged guilty. He stood before those He loved and listened as they shouted, "Crucify!" Jesus the Son of God looked into the eyes of those He loved as He lifted His cross. He made His way, dusty step by dusty step while they mocked and jeered and taunted. Step by step then stumble. Was it under the weight of the timber to which He would soon be nailed? Was it because of the pain from beatings and whippings already endured? Or was it the sound of jeering voices, and the sight of mocking faces? Step after step up to the summit of the hill where He would be hung to die. So many faces of those He loved beyond measure lining the route. Face after face looking back with hate-filled eyes, spitting in the face of their loving Saviour.

As the nails pierced His hands and feet, did He call upon the wrath of God? Did He call upon His Father to save Him and punish those who stood against Him? No. As metal was hammered through flesh and presses bone against wood, His cries were on our behalf. What love. What miraculous love beyond our comprehension. As blood flowed along the grains of timber His cry of, "Father forgive them, for they know not what they do" (Luke 23:34) was heard above the clamour. It must be the ultimate demonstration of love. In that moment, all the wonder, all the beauty, all the greatness and all the goodness of this world was far surpassed. Every good thing was far exceeded by the love of our Saviour as He cried out on behalf of those inflicting pain on Him, those intent on killing Him. And death came. Jesus did die for us. He died for each and every one of us past, present and future. He died so that we can live. Pain beyond our imagination. Love beyond our grasp. Death and resurrection so that we can live to the full, just as we were originally created.

A shoulder strap creaks intermittently, in time with my own erratic steps. My legs are tired, and shoulders sore from carrying the heavy backpack. It is hard going over rough ground. Under this weight any small hurdle becomes a barrier. That peat hag, too high to step onto, and too high to jump off. This stream, too wide to jump across. That boulder, too far to reach with a single stride.

But there it is: the summit up ahead. Buckles released, rucksack is lain on the ground. Now I feel as though I am floating. I move off feeling light, feeling free. I start to run because I can. Now the weight of the rucksack is removed, I feel as though I could run endlessly over this terrain. Long strides over rough ground. The pleasure of moving fast and moving light. Another stream, now quickly crossed in a single jump. From boulder to boulder, over rises and dips and on toward the summit.

The ground here is no easier than before. In fact it is harder. The wind is blowing stronger. Boulders are bigger, streams more frequent. But my rucksack is off, so I keep running, smiling, running free. Ready to face up to and overcome whatever obstacle this route will bring.

When we give our lives to God, accepting that Jesus died to cover our sin, we are relieved of a burden. The death we once faced because of our sin was a serious burden. No amount of work would free us from it. Getting rid of it would cost more than we could ever afford, until Jesus came and paid it for us. Now we are released to step into the freedom that has been bought for us. "It is for freedom that Christ has set us free. Stand firm, then, and do not let yourselves be burdened again by a yoke of slavery" (Galatians 5:1). We are free from slavery. We are free from the binds of religiosity and from working for salvation. We are free from the heavy burden of sin. The moment we hand our lives to God, that burden is off and left behind us. That moment we acknowledge that Jesus is the King of kings, our Saviour, our Hero, and we ask God to dwell within us through His Holy Spirit, we step into the ultimate freedom.

"Now the Lord is the Spirit, and where the Spirit of the Lord is, there is freedom. And we who with

unveiled faces all reflect the Lord's glory, are being
transformed into his likeness with ever-increasing
glory, which comes from the Lord, who is the
Spirit"

(2 Corinthians 3:17&18)

From the moment we give our lives to God, we can walk
in freedom, bringing glory to God, by being transformed into
Christ's likeness.

We live to emulate our Saviour, our King, the greatest
hero to have ever walked this earth. We live a life shaped by
the knowledge that we are headed to a place of wonder that
far surpasses our wildest dreams. We live a life of praise, a
life of freedom. We live a life of Christ-likeness. Like Him,
and because of Him we know who we are and why we are
here. We know where we are headed. Like Him we can walk
with God in wild places free from all the distractions. Like
Jesus we can kneel in corners of wild creation and revel
in the fact that nature in all its grandeur is just a hint of
the wonders to come. We can surround ourselves with wild
creation and understand more fully than ever that eternal
life stretches out before us. We can draw near to our Father
because Jesus has bridged the gap between our Creator and
us. He has relieved us of our burdens and set us free. He has
set us free to be ourselves.

Life will still bring its hardships and difficulties. In fact
it may even seem like there are more, but now with the All
Powerful God beside us, our yoke is easy and our burden
light (Matthew 11:30). We now face them in a new way,
with a new determination and with a new readiness. We can
face them, standing tall, being open and free and natural,
without the added effort of keeping masks in place. We are
unveiled and real; we are people of integrity. We can face
the hardships in the knowledge that the battle is already
won. We are, as Paul writes,

"more than conquerors through him who loved
us. For... neither death nor life, neither angels nor
demons, neither present nor the future, nor any

powers, neither height nor depth, nor anything else
in all creation, will be able to separate us from the
love of God that is in Jesus Christ our Lord"
(Romans 8:37-39).

We can choose to live fully and wonderfully if we bring
ourselves before God and seek the answers to our biggest
questions. We can know who we are, why we are here and
where we are going.

"You have made known to me the path of life; you
will fill me with joy in your presence, with eternal
pleasures at your right hand"
(Psalm 16:11)

We are a dwelling place for God and He knows the full
plan for our lives.

"O Lord... you know me. You know when I sit and
when I rise. You discern my going out and my lying
down; you are familiar with all my ways. Before a
word is on my tongue you know it completely, O
Lord"
(Psalm 139:1-4)

God the creator of the universe knows us more than we
know ourselves. He is intensely interested in every little
detail of our lives, what we do, what we say and where we
go. He has a perfect plan for our lives. He sent His son to
die for us so that we can live out this plan to its fullest.
What incredible love! What glorious freedom we have been
granted. Accepting what Jesus has done means we are set
free to live a life radically different from that which we have
known before. It is like the difference between living in full
warming sunlight rather than cold damp shadows. Like the
difference between vibrant white and murky grey. Between
standing tall or cowering away. The difference between a
white torrent as rain falls, and a muddy trickle in times of
drought. We are set free to live a life that is vibrant and
full.

Between A Rock & A Momentarily Hard Place
(Freedom From Short-Term Thinking)

'We only live life once, but if we live it right then once is enough.'   (Red Allen)

She runs and runs and jumps and runs. Unafraid. Free. Exploring the vast natural world around her. Adara, my little daughter. Her name means 'To see beauty', and it is well chosen. Run, jump, pause, stare. Knit together in her mother's womb. Known by God before her parents. Known by God completely. Created by Him, now she looks around and sees His beauty. Where will she go? What path will she follow in this life that stretches out before her? One in which she will always see the beauty is my prayer for her. Her life must seem endless from her young perspective. As vast as this wild world around her.

The stone she throws splashes into the fast-flowing water. Between the most innocent laughs she looks for more stones to throw. Stone after stone pass beneath the waters surface to join all the others on the cold riverbed. Stone after stone disappear as quickly as the years will. As fast as the river flows over the rocks below, so will the years of her life flow. As have my years. So quickly they pass. And years from now this riverside walk will seem like just yesterday. Adara, only two years old, sunlight turning her fairest hair to glimmering-gold. Her laughter joining the birdsong and ringing through the trees. Years from now this will all be like yesterday.

I watch as her boundless energy carries her away from the riverside and off along the path. Her explorers' eyes spot the old tree-stump. What compels her to climb it I do not know. But climb it she does. Another laugh. Hands on hips, she owns the world. This vast world spreading out all around her. Natural beauty of wild creation matched by her own. But so quickly she falls. One moment on top, the next she is tumbling down. Lindsay reaches her first and helps her to her feet. Not even a cry and off she goes again.

I watch Lindsay as she watches Adara. The mother - child connection is so powerful, so strong, so right and true and pure. I watch Lindsay and think how difficult it is to believe that physical beauty is a passing thing. Today Lindsay seems more beautiful than yesterday. Yesterday she seemed more beautiful than the day before. That day more so than the one before it. And so on, right back to that first moment I saw her all those years ago. That moment when I had thought her more beautiful than anyone I had ever seen.

Now together we walk through the years, and through many wild places. Now together we watch as our daughter grows. Together we three make memories that will endure throughout our lives. So many experiences Adara has had already. So many still to come. Such a long life it must seem that stretches out before her. Smiling we walk along the path. Smiling we walk through the years.

Are you making the most of your life?

Get out into wild places and face your own mortality. Realise the shortness of your years on this earth. Get out and say like the Psalmist "O Lord... let me know how fleeting is my life. You have made my days a mere handbreadth; the span of my life is as nothing before you. Each man's life is but a breath" (Psalm 39:4&5). Stand amidst natural creation and realise how transient your rapidly ageing body is. See how the world around is ageing and realise that in terms of timescales, it's ageing process dwarves our whole life span. Get out, look around at a world of impermanence and face the inevitable.

By getting out of the routines of every day life we do face our own mortality. Yet our short life is of utmost and eternal significance, for Jesus came and saved us from the power of the grave. It is not our physical body that will live forever, but our spirit. For our bodies will age and die and decay and return to the earth, and we will be 'clothed in a new spiritual body' (1 Corinthians 15:42-54). And this short life will determine how that eternity will be spent. God has made a way. Our life is short, but God loves us enough and cares for us enough that He made a way for life to continue. Death is not the end. "O Lord, what is man that you care for him, the son of man that you think of him? Man is like a breath; his days are like a fleeting shadow." (Psalm 144:3-5).

Jesus came and died for us so that we may live. We can look death in the face and smile, knowing that it is just the next stage of the journey. Out in the natural world the inevitability of death is not glossed over. In realising the shortness of our earthly lifetime we can find the release to be who we are meant to be today. Our focus rapidly shifts from short-term perspective to the eternal. Living with an eternal perspective is absolutely liberating. It means stepping fully into the freedom of life with Christ. Standing in a natural setting and being reminded of our eternal God means that we can be freed to act differently in our time here, whilst shaping our eternity.

Many times among hills and mountains and forests and valleys I have found my mind shifting subconsciously onto the subject of death. Set in the context of my faith it is a wonderful experience. I return feeling more free to live fully and with less concern about the worldly consequences. Life-changing experiences are a wonderful thing. These revelations of how fleeting our earthly life is, and of the eternity before me, are times that have changed me. 'Before' and 'after' points in my life. One such memory is of an experience one wet weekend on the misty, rocky island of Skye.

All had gone so well on the first day's long walk in from the South side of the mighty Cullin mountains. The Skye Bridge had carried us to the island and we abandoned the van at the end of a single-track road. From there we set off on foot, in fine weather and even finer spirits. After a lunch stop and a brief glimpse at the map we started ascending the rock-strewn slopes up and onto the rim of a fantastically remote little corrie. It contained a small loch framed on three sides by sheer rock faces. Whilst pitching our tent we paused regularly to listen to the echoes of various words and statements dreamed up specifically for echo production. For Simon in particular it seemed that this activity would keep him amused all evening. I believe had he been there alone, the sound of his laughter following his own echoing voice would still have filled the corrie!

During the night the rain fell and inside became as wet as outside. Cold soon penetrated our shelter as easily as the water. Peals of thunder echoed off the rocky walls and ensured that even if the discomfort of cold, wet, cramped conditions could be overcome, sleep would still be regularly interrupted. The flashes of lightning lit the inside of the tent and revealed the open eyes of Ross and Simon, neither any closer to sleep than I was. Eventually morning did arrive and the only thing we could do was get out of bed, scramble into cold soaking clothes and run about to build up some heat. The cloud that surrounded us allowed only a view of a few metres before rock and cloud merged to vaguely differing shades of the same.

Upon reaching the ridge it seemed that there was no way to progress along it in either direction. The only way seemed down the other side, some number of miles and summits West or 'left' from where we planned! To either side of us loomed steep rock walls that seemed impossible to climb without ropes and harnesses. Another problem lay in the fact that the way down was unknown and this gave rise to the fear that we would find ourselves in trouble. Simon of course showed no fear and with some dry joke about 'becoming mountain statistics' set off into the unknown, showing as little interest in democratic decision, as he did concern for the predicament. At this time his humour seemed to be the only dry thing in a world of wetness. Ross sat looking as unhappy as the grey around us and stated that there was no way he was taking that route. While I tried to convince him that staying together was the safest option, Simon disappeared into the cloud. It wasn't until his infectious laugh echoed up the gully that Ross decided to follow his totalitarian lead. We knew of course that the laughter did not mean a safe route had been found - but more likely another echo spot - yet it was a sound that somehow lightened the situation.

I too set off into the steep gully, dropping from rock to rock, trying to avoid starting any rolling toward Ross and Simon somewhere below. To my left rose a continuous line of vertical rock – the kind of rock that Hamish Brown, the first man to complete all the Munros in a single walk, would refer to as "the very bones of creation laid bare". I paused and stared, for it suddenly struck me how hard the rock appeared, not in terms of how easy it would be to climb, but in terms of its physical structure. It sounds strange but it felt as though I had never really considered the hardness of rock before, nor grasped its age in this way. On my other side, rock walls again filled my view, and now I was struck not by their hardness but by their friability, for at each glance I saw cracks and fissures and pieces of precariously positioned loose rock that evoked the sensation that I was not in a hard place, but a place that was ageing just the same as any living being. The sense of age only increased and for a brief moment it felt as though I was getting a sense of the age of my surroundings. The rock somehow inspired an appreciation, and a sense of deep respect for eternity and the Creator who had been there and will be there throughout - the "Living God, the eternal King" (Jeremiah 10:10). It was in relation to this thought that I became more aware of how the whole earth was ageing almost as fast as I was. It seemed almost as fragile as flesh and bone, despite moments before having seemed so very solid and lasting. Now it seemed that any hardness was momentary. I was hit with the blatant reality that life is entirely pointless if it is lived only for the here and now, if it is lived within no bigger context. The result was not a sense of despair but one of liberation. I soon caught up with my two friends on what had turned out to be a safe route down. I was sure that if they looked close enough they would see a glow on my face like that of Moses after his encounter with God.

"Live, don't doubt, praise and lift a shout out,
Ask for time, but time is lost on memories passed,
Day by day, cast your cares away,
Ask for time, but time is pointless when I'm here in your hands.

Time passes by, years passing by, hours passing by,
But you didn't pass me by.

And you're all around me; You're everywhere I look,
And put your arms around me, You're everywhere I am,

Lower my guard, dance in my Heart,
Don't ask for time, cos time is worthless when I'm held in your arms."

(Andy Dorrat, 'A Thousand Years', 2005)

In that moment on the rocky mountain slopes, I had been intensely aware that it would be a moment I would not forget. And I had felt aware of my lifetime and the decades it would span here on earth, and how I would look back on those too from an eternal future. Describing the experience is difficult, for like all revelation, it was made up of sensation and emotion as much as it was thought. So much of the world around us seems to lean toward glossing over this issue of the transience of our life. Death itself is often a taboo subject. Millions of pounds are poured into cosmetic, surgical and medical research aimed at slowing down or preventing the ageing process in a vain attempt to keep people looking young and in their prime. Death is one of the few inevitable events in our life yet so much effort goes into hiding the fact that the years are carrying us rapidly toward it.

So often amidst the busyness of everyday life it seems possible to forget the blatant fact that we are mortal. Death comes to all of us and yet, when it does, it seems to cause surprise for those close to the person. People ask questions, 'Why could medicine not save him?' 'How could the doctors let her die?' Or 'How could God let that happen?' We all die; it is one of the few inevitable things we face in our short life. Walk down a busy street on a sunny afternoon. Look at all the people wandering along, shopping bags swinging in their hands. Look at them - many dressed like the models in the shop windows displaying the latest fashions. See the children running about laughing. And the old people on benches watching the world drift by and reminiscing about 'the good old times'! Every one of these people are progressing rapidly toward death. No exceptions. Rarely does this thought cross our minds in such a place though, and it is even more rare that you would hear it as the topic of conversation. It is glossed over by the constant focus on the here and now and the high value that is placed on immediate rewards.

Another rock falls away. It tumbles and spins a long way before striking a larger boulder with such force that it shatters to countless jagged pieces. Now, in the ensuing silence, my mind spins like the rock. It spins as I consider how long that rock had sat there in that particular position before my boot had set it rolling. How many years, decades, centuries had it taken for those colourful lichens to cover its surface? How many more years would it be before slow-growing lichens cover the newly shattered pieces, and before

*another foot or hoof or flood would set them moving? Had
it once been connected to the large cliff standing up ahead
before falling downwards to form this scree-slope? Had they
all once been connected, one huge solid monolith of rock at
the beginning of time? When God said 'Let there be light', did
it reveal this place as smooth and solid, as yet unaffected by
erosion and age?*

When thinking of timescales that we cannot fully grasp,
or when considering eternal matters, suddenly the whole of
human history relating to wild places can seem brief. It is
possible to imagine whole lives, whole generations, and whole
eras like snapshots. Just the shortest glimmer of each and
then it is gone, and the next one, and the one after that, all
gone in a strobe-like haze. Each flicker revealing a variation
on the previous so that a whole segment of recorded history
is gone in seconds in relation to the deep unfathomable time
of eternity.

In one flicker we might see Abraham led by God to the
wild mountain spot where he prepares to sacrifice his only
son. We hear as Abraham calls to God 'the eternal God'
(Genesis 21:33), and God rewards him for his faith. Then
Abraham is gone and many of the generations that follow
him, gone in the briefest of flickers when set against the
unfathomable backdrop of eternity.

Flicker –David is roaming the wilderness learning many
of the great skills that would lead him to the greatest of
kingships. We watch briefly as David finds his soul restored
through meeting with God, being led by Him beside quiet
waters, being made to lie down in green pastures. We could
watch as he writes his many psalms, recording the greatness
of God that he saw revealed through His creation. Those
words live on but King David has gone to be with the King
of Kings, our God Eternal.

Flicker – there is the voice from the wilderness preparing
the way. John living off locusts and honey away from the
polluting effects of society. Preparing himself to prepare
others. All that preparation, all those words of power, the

numerous baptisms - all gone. Snuffed out so quickly as the blade comes down upon his neck.

Flicker – even Jesus' life on earth, is relatively short, and yet of utmost significance. There are the miracles; the teaching and the regular solo walks into the wilder corners of His father's creation. There is the transfiguration high on the slopes of Mount Hermon, and there's the feeding of the 5000 on the wild slopes above the Sea of Galilee. This flicker would reveal just how central a role the wilderness would play in Jesus' short ministry. So suddenly this light is snuffed out by the brutal hands of the men He came to save. And here though is the point that separates Jesus from all the others, for Jesus rises from death, transcending all eras, past, present and future. Living so that we too may choose this life eternal.

Flicker – now we see a world that has changed, where people are either followers of Christ or not, where time itself is divided into before and after His death. People are forming new churches and new orders. There are the Celts on their islands and remote monasteries being inspired by and knowing their Father through His creation. See them, as they watch patiently the waves breaking on the coasts and whales swimming past. In scenes like these the Celtic understanding of divine love is enhanced and they are inspired to communicate it through creative ways. The legacy of Celtic poetry and art and literature is the suitable result. Watch St. Cuthbert there in Scotland as he learns from the wilds of the Island of Lindisfarne. Across the inspirational sea to Ireland, and watch St. Patrick roaming the rolling land. See his forty-day fast on the mountains. Then St. Columba upon his Island hill, sitting on a crest of a rock, watching the swells of the sea and listening as they 'chant music to their Father everlastingly.'* And like a light snuffed out this whole era is gone and all that is left are the tales of their times. Silence that now rests where poems and prayers once rang out.

* From a poem attributed to St. Columba.

Flicker – there is Francis roaming the hills and meadows of the high Tuscan countryside round Assisi. His example is so powerful and so in tune with the beautiful countryside and its creator that he leaves a strong and lasting legacy behind after his short flash of life. Through the beauty of the landscape and a vivid grasp of the eternal perspective we would see that Francis finds little trouble in giving all his belongings to the poor, even the cloak off his back. We see his followers grouping, and even a monastic order forming. Look on as other Franciscans learn, through time spent in prayer surrounded by the rugged beauty of the Tuscan landscape, to live simply and selflessly, with their mind fixed upon their eternal home. Then Francis is gone. The flame is out and all that is left is a version of his order and a life story that continues to inspire millions.

Flicker – it's the era of exploration with people mapping and conquering the hills in the name of science. Man has stood on the highest peak, Chomolungma (Everest), and expeditions set out to the far-flung corners of the world. We would see many of these explorers having life-changing spiritual experiences as they pursue their explorative goals and record having met with God through the order found in the creation they study.

Flicker – now here we are, roaming the hills, ascending them with ropes and axes, descending them on skis and paragliders all in keeping with the era of recreation. A quick weekend fix is the name of the game before returning to the high-tech lives of the third millennium. There are still some finding this place a site of spiritual exercise where much can be learned of what lies beyond. There are still some who shout about the benefits of meeting God in His wild landscapes. But soon they too will simply be gone in a flicker. When we join all these historical figures in heaven, what legacy will be left beyond the short flash of our lives?

The hot air swirls around us, scented strongly with Jasmine and a whole array of wild flowers. Flowers of every description. Flowers of such intimate detail that they defy description, and each infusing the air with a scent of its own. Here in this Italian mountainous environment colourful blooms are in profusion. Colour and aroma everywhere. Beauty at every glance. A smile with every inhalation. No more beautiful than our Celtic homeland - just different.

Now flower scent fades away, as does the hot air. Cool air scented with damp earth and wet rock emanates from somewhere deep within the mountain. Great wafts of it pushing out from the dark inner reaches beyond our sight. Out from within the chasm that the water has worn into the very rock of which the landscape is comprised. We proceed into the mountain, great smooth walls of limestone rising on either side. Hair swept back and faces and clothes dampened by the cool mist-laden air pushing out past us through the gap.

The roar grows louder. We shout above its din. We can taste the damp as we arrive at the balcony; a balcony wide enough for us to stand and stare. A balcony within the mountain, and before us, soft white water cascades from an unseen valley high above, and plunges vertically to smash into a pool far below. The whole waterfall can be seen from our viewpoint at roughly mid-height. The white water pouring over the lip above glimmers in the sunlight and through some visual trick seems to pause for the briefest moment before plunging down and down to stir the already turbulent waters of the pool below. The pool is struck with such force that mist of the finest droplets rises rapidly, forced up along with the cool air. It rises, and as it does it passes through thin rays of sunlight that have squeezed through holes and gaps in the narrow gorge above making lasers of light and mist appear to shoot out of the pool far below. They shoot up past our balcony and through a thin rainbow that arcs across the chasm.

Over aeons of time that soft white water has cut this chasm. How many have gazed upon this wonder? How many of those lives have now passed? How many were impacted by its force and wonder? How many more will be impacted in the future? How many have been struck by the timescales this creative process requires? Timescales that dwarf our own and reveal it as a mere shadow passing over this land.

Outside the tunnel we read the sign. 'Four millimetres per year', it claims. Four millimetres of rock, carved and worn away and swept rapidly toward the depths of Lake Garda just a few kilometres away. The rock walls loom above and the impact of that fact hits with almost as much force as the water hitting the pool in the murky depths. Like stirred waters, so are emotions moved. To stand and look at that ribbon of white water we had passed through at least thirty meters of rock that had been cut by its flowing action. In my lifetime that water will have smoothed away a mere 120 millimetres of rock. In Lindsay's a little less. And in Adara's lifetime only eight millimetres of rock will have been carved. We could visit this place throughout our lives and even on our hundredth birthday it would look much as it does now. Yet there it is before us. The deep chasm of water-worn rock, a chasm created at a pace we cannot even see.

Emerging from the misty half-light and back into daylight and scented air our mist-covered faces glisten, and smiles stretch wide. Adara says "Water, crash, water, crash". Lindsay says she feels she has a clearer understanding of the power and splendour of God. Adara repeats "Water crash", and I walk along grinning and know exactly what they mean.

The mountains and wild areas have endured over vast periods of time and this sense of timelessness draws many towards them. Yet even the mountains come and go like those who walk upon them. Even they are just a flicker in a grander scale. When faced with this kind of thinking we can realise more fully how totally insignificant we are without God and yet we can feel a sense of utter freedom because our relationship with Christ entitles us to step into eternity. It is hard to believe that with eternity lying before us we should worry about small or petty things. How pathetic it is when my concern for what people will think of me prevents me from compelling them to come to know their God. I worry that speaking the name of Jesus may offend someone despite the fact that with Him, his or her life could be so utterly enhanced. When I am on a hill, or exploring a rock strewn valley, impacted with this sense of deep time, then my reluctance with such matters, my hesitations on speaking the name of Jesus are revealed as ridiculous to the point of being shameful. It feels as though creation ignites such feelings, like the cockerel crowing for the third time - every time. Such is the power of the contemplation of time amongst creation. When we realise that the whole of that seemingly solid but ageing creation is just another flicker against the backdrop of eternity, it is hard not to return changed, and it is change that we should welcome.

> "The cross is the focal point of history and this wonderful gospel of ours makes the past incredibly relevant, gives us a glorious future and fills the present with meaning, purpose and adventure. As regards the future, we are not looking ahead with a sense of escapism. We look to the future to give us inspiration and motivation for the present. If you know Jesus, you can look forward to a tremendous future and be inspired by the truth that you will spend eternity with Him. It is that inspiration that fuels the present."
> (Lenny Turk, 'Yesterday, Today, Forever')

When we realise the real context into which our life is placed, then we are set free to live in the present to the absolute full. My father-in-law, who knows the joy to be found in meeting with God in wild places, spoke the words, quoted above, during a sermon on the subject of time. He preached the word of God, and afterwards life seemed positively different. He spoke about how the past and the future through our relationship with our Father release us to live fully in the present. He explained that, as Christians, we do not look to the past for any nostalgic reason but because it is of central importance to our life today. Through the cross alone we have a glorious future and our focus on that impacts upon our present. This is what we can experience in the wild, when we realise that even the natural world that surrounds us is so impermanent. We can believe more fully that the cross has set us free from the fear of death. We can believe that we are progressing toward a glorious eternal life with Jesus who died for us. The result is that we live our lives in the present fully for Him, in the freedom that His love has given us. We can run free in the present with the chains of death lying in a weak crumpled pile behind us.

The snowflake falls silently to land with the gentlest touch upon the earth. From the towering grey cloud it comes and, together with others, transforms the world to white. Its delicate structure rests upon frozen land. Others drift down and land beside it, around it, on top of it. No two the same. All delicate. All light. All translucent white. But all unique. My feet compress these flakes together. Each step making a muffled crunching noise as the snow compacts beneath my weight. Snow continues to fall heavily. A strange description, given the lightness of each part. Yet the sum of these parts has a strength way beyond my own. In comfort I sit as it moulds around my body. My body is tired after the long climb. Below me the snow, now well compacted, has turned to solid ice. Like the ice of ages past when snow fell and fell and fell and compressed the layers below. Thick sheets of ice that stretched out across the land. Thick sheets of ice harder than the land below. Gravity moved it over this land, this very land where I now sit. The great boulders and pieces of rock it dragged, acted like teeth ploughing the land. Gravity pulled this great plough as it sculpted the land below, as it gouged out this valley, like an ox or horse or tractor pulls a plough to make furrows in a field. On the slopes of this furrow I now sit, dwarfed by its scale, a humbled speck in its vastness. The ice is long gone, but this thin layer of snow covers a land that is still being shaped, still ageing, still being eroded over vast incomprehensible timescales.

Snow-clouds have gone and have been replaced by swirling mist. Tiny particles of moisture swirl with the air as I move further down the valley. The solid rock I am gripping onto feels cold and wet. The cracks, into which I plunge my cold fingers, searching for a secure hold, are as wet as the more exposed stone. As night moves in, the temperature drops. Cloudless skies retain no heat and all that is wet soon freezes. The moisture in the cracks freezes and as it does it expands. I rub the tiny particles of moisture between my finger and thumb and watch them soak away to nothing. I look at the wet rock and consider how the moisture, and the effect of freezing, can push the rock apart. Tiny particles of moisture that, over time, match the power of any chisel. Smooth, solid rock split into jagged pieces.

With the morning comes the rain. Droplets fall to land with a splash, joining those that have previously fallen. The puddles have overflowed in trickles to become a flowing mass. The silver droplets join together as though attracted to each other by some unseen force, then they run like mercury beads, to drip from my clothes onto the sodden ground below. Some soak away into the peaty ground and then seep into dark subterranean channels. Pure and clear it springs from the ground on the slopes of the valley lower down. Other droplets flow from trickle to burn and burn to river as momentum and volume increase. It follows this river course as it sweeps away the earth, and leaves only boulders and solid rock in place. Yet even these rocks succumb, over time, to shaping. As the water flows around and over and against, it smoothes and shapes and pushes. A swell of water shifts a rock, and it crashes to a stop against another. The particles of stone broken off are carried by the river flow. The water continues its cutting course from summit-heights to sea. Cutting ever deeper into the ground over which it flows. Cutting ever deeper into the earth, it sculpts rock and perpetually shapes the land.

A tiny fragment of stone tumbles and turns. A small particle that was once part of a great towering cliff, then a jagged rock, then a smooth pebble. Now it moves through bubbles and amongst boulders as it is carried from stream to sea. Tidal-forces replace river flow. Tidal-forces that push the particle onto the beach where it joins countless others. Each has its own story, its own journey. Particles once part of crags and cliffs and boulders and mountains. Mountains that slowly crumble and erode and are eventually broken

*down and carried off to sea, there to be swept and battered
by the waves that endlessly lap against and shape the shore
of this ageing land. The waves crash against the boundaries
established at creation. Foundations of a world set by an
infinite God, whose awesomeness my finite mind can grasp
but a fraction. Boundaries and foundations of the world still
being shaped by processes He created.*

*And so from the vast surface of the seas moisture rises to
form great billowing clouds. Clouds that are carried by the
wind toward the distant land. Moisture that condenses as
the air rises over the mighty mountains. I watch the towering
clouds approach. How much water does each hold? How will
it fall? A gentle snowflake? A single drop of rain? Moisture
to form a mist across the land? What effect will it have on
the land toward which it moves? Where will its journey end?
When will this process cease?*

Time does another strange thing in natural settings. It
seems to stop! It was one of those rare clear days where lunch
is possible on the summit without feeling cold in seconds.
It was a poignant moment for my friend Calum, being his
first Munro since a kidney transplant a year earlier. He was
now living life to the full, working, playing and living life
adventurously, making up for the time he had lost to dialysis.
A radical change of career saw him giving up a well paid job
to go and work for little more than his keep, leading young
people in outdoor activities, and in doing so, seeing many
hand their lives over to God. It was he who first noticed that
day, that time, like our surroundings, had frozen. The pause
button had been hit on the controls of our busy lives.

While chewing and slurping, we discussed the pace of
life; the way days and weeks fly by and become part of the
past so quickly. We could look down and see lives carrying
on as normal. Cars hurtling along the valley roads. Houses
here and there. With binoculars we could probably have
seen the car we had left and the footsteps leading uphill
away from it. Already the ascent was but a memory, a thing
of the past. We discussed how it felt as though we had been
plucked from our lives and placed here where we could assess

them. We were plucked out of time and our lives down there were on pause. It is perhaps the best way to see what things we have given too much priority and what we have given too little. What unnecessary pressures have we placed on ourselves? What schedules are we striving to meet and yet are really of no consequence? Out in natural places, out of routine life, is where these things can be brought before God and put in order.

Each time I have experienced this impact upon my sense of time, it feels like a moment when I am most fully alive. It is an experience available to all of us. It is in such places that, rather than dreaming about the future or thinking about schedules or deadlines, we can simply find ourselves *being*. The sorting out of a busy life is not a conscious process, but a by-product of being fully alive knowing that our relationship with God is the thing of utmost importance. Stepping back from our lives can have the effect of helping us to see everything clearer. It does not have to be a complicated thing; a lot of the time it is just instinctive. Deep down we know the things that are really important to us. Time away from the routines and schedules allows time to assess our life, and when we acknowledge the things of most importance, that is when we can start to live life to the full. These moments impact and even define the rest of our life. Life is different afterwards because we have gained a new, or altered perspective. Life, and the adventure it is, can be enjoyed more fully because in God we will have found significance and tasted full life as He intended. It is perhaps what John Muir discovered during his 'three year Sabbath' in Yosemite. After some wild experience he felt that it is something everyone should feel and be changed by. "Time spent in the wild will enhance your life", he stated, going on to say, "Give a month at least to this precious reserve. The time will not be taken from the sum of your life. Instead of shortening, it will indefinitely lengthen it." Life certainly has seemed longer for me when viewed from these timeless places. Our time on earth still seems but a flicker, but the fact that eternity starts right now impacts our whole life. It seems that these short moments of contemplation stretch, as does life accordingly. Perhaps it is simply that time is taken to appreciate it. I know it is why so many lunches in wild places can be eaten side by side in a most comfortable silence. The sweet flavour brought to life through a deepening of our relationship with the God of Ages is utterly satisfying.

This is an opportunity not to be missed. Get out there and contemplate the past. Contemplate the tremendous significance of the cross. Consider the future, our life eternal, and be released to live fully in the present. We need a healthy view of time. Don't get consumed or dwell on past things. Don't be fearful of the future or cower from death. Live life to the full. Next time you are hesitant to speak the name of Jesus you'll think back to the rocks or wild place that brought revelation of time. Next time your life feels hectic you'll long for that wild seat where God gives the gift of perspective. Thank God for His peace and these places where He infuses us with it. Just take the opportunity to get out there once in a while and contemplate your place in time. Take time to stop every so often and ask yourself whether you're so busy living life focused on some fleeting thing or other that you're forgetting to really live. It may be the next weekend, the next holiday, shopping spree, new car, career goal; whatever it is, stop and consider what importance you are placing on it. These things are not bad in themselves, only when they start to consume us because of the excessive importance we place on them. Living life with an eternal perspective is what every Christian professes to do. This arena where the concept of time is radically altered is a chance for all of us to develop our understanding of the eternity we face. Through this increased understanding we can return with a healthy disregard for all the momentary things that blind us to real eternal perspective. It is as though scales are removed from our eyes so that the hazy future that we put our faith in becomes as clear as an icy mountain stream flowing over pure granite, and all the glittering materials and short-term dreams fade. As a result we will be bolder, caring only for God's desire for our life. We will be swayed less in the tides and currents and trends of society. We will be more fully separated from the world because we are truly living a radical life in light of eternity. We will live confidently, bringing glory to God and knowing more fully than ever that 'To live is Christ, to die is gain.' To live is to do so fully and wonderfully, Spirit filled and complete thanks to the sacrifice of Jesus. To die is to pass into the incredible eternity in a place of unimaginable wonder.

It has been a long windy walk over many summits. Now tired legs carry me slowly back to where it started. Down the slope I descend, the long drop back to the valley floor. Down from the rocky windswept heights and over the browns of the heather carpet. Down through waist-deep bracken to the welcomed green of the trees, their branches outstretched like arms ready to embrace. They seem to welcome me in, then wave the wind away. Under their canopy the air is stiller, a place of peace and quiet after the continuous buffeting of the wind.

I sit to rest against this great oak stump. Under the carpet of leaves its roots spread out beneath me. Roots that had held its great weight in place through many wild storms. Alongside me lie the remnants of the trunk, its limbs broken off, leaves long gone. Bark falls away in plates as the whole structure decays and returns to the ground from which it came. I feel my muscles stiffening already. I know I will be sore tomorrow. Sunny Sunday afternoon walks as a child with my family seem like just yesterday. Walks in places just like this. Running wild with my sister, while my other sister lies in her pram. Running wild with seemingly endless energy until the car journey home when all would be silent in the back. Then each of us carried from car to bed in the arms of our parents. Next day though, we would rise early again, full of energy, recharged, ready for another day of wild adventure. Not now though. I will rise tomorrow, and I suppose I could push myself to do the same long walk again, but I would feel the ache in my muscles. I would feel pain in my joints. Somewhere among the years it has changed, my body has aged. Years that have passed like days. Now I am the one in the front of the car. Now Lindsay and I carry Adara to bed after she has spent her energy running wild in wild places, throwing stones in rivers, exploring woodlands, and climbing sand-dunes.

As I sit against this stump, looking at the fallen tree, how much longer will it be, I wonder, until these long summit walks are just a memory? Will they seem like just yesterday as shuffling steps and a stick grasped in shaky hands carries me falteringly along the pavement? I'm sure I will grin at a life well spent. I'm sure I will grin as I approach my final summit in whatever form it comes. That summit I have been heading inevitably toward all my life. I will smile the widest of smiles as I raise my eyes from earth to heaven, knowing that this time there will be no descent. I will smile as never before as I take my first steps off that summit and into the arms of the one who awaits. My first joyous steps into the realm of the eternal.

Ascend To Transcend
(Freedom From Norms And Expectations)

Water emerges from rock high upon the mountain slopes. It emerges clear, pure and filtered by its journey through subterranean channels, and by its slow seeping into and through the porous rock. Now, from the darkness it emerges into light, ready to start its journey along a predetermined course. A journey marked out by the shape of the land. The land that lies between these summit heights and the vast depths of the ocean. On steep slopes the journey begins, just a trickle, but flowing fast.

In the womb a child is formed. Life from the moment of conception. Knit together, formed, loved by its Creator before its parents even know it. In the womb, an explosion of creative energy. In the darkness, life anew. A soul unique from any other. A heartbeat soon develops and human form takes shape. Then from the darkness it emerges and the lungs are filled with air. A course is set for the child to follow. It is a fulfilling course that will take them from beginning to end, filled with meaning and purpose, then into the arms of their loving heavenly Father: The Father who has set the course, ordained life, and offered an eternal home, if they will just follow the course.

Down the slopes the water flows, gathering momentum and force. More water trickles down the burn sides, drips off overhanging rocks, seeps through valley-sides or falls directly from the clouds above. It continues to grow in volume and speed, cascading over rocks, flowing over boulders, plunging over edges, through the rapids and into deep pools. Ever flowing. Ever moving. Ever following the course to the vast open sea.

Rapidly the child develops. They grow with a thirst for knowledge. They learn through watching those around them. They learn through exploration of their environment, through books, and experiences and observations. Learning, always learning. Always adding to the knowledge already obtained. Learning and choosing, deciding now where their life will go. Deciding which paths to take in a life with many crossroads.

White water cascades over rocks then slows as it spreads out into the deep. It is not the deep of the sea or loch, but that of a reservoir. A vast volume of water pushes against a curving concrete wall. Its energy is harnessed, suppressed, and its flow is altered. Pipelines carry it away. Carry it away toward turbines that are turned by force. The harnessed energy is turned into electricity and along with the water it is carried off towards the city lights and thirsty lives. The river flow is diverted from its original course. Below the concrete walls flows just a trickle. It seeps feebly into the ground beneath sun-bleached rocks and stones. Rocks and stones once smoothed and shaped and polished by the river flow until all the energy was harnessed and redirected. Until it was diverted away from the original course.

How is your life being shaped?

Have the dreams you once had been altered, repressed, ignored, buried? Have you found yourself living a life of mundane routines and habits? Do you remember a time when every day was lived to the full? Have you had a time in your life when anything seemed possible, and nothing could stop you? Is life still lived to the full? Or do you just get by?

I have seen people getting worn out following paths that are not meant for them. I have been on those paths myself. Paths that drain away the energy like water seeping through sand. I remember the feeling, and what it is like to hear the ring of the alarm, to hit the snooze button and lie wishing for any other day to be stretching out before me than the one that was. I know what it is like to swing my legs out of bed and sit up slowly, trying to find the motivation for the day ahead. It is not easy to spend what little energy you feel you have left on a pursuit that feels so futile. I have spoken to too many others who relate to these feelings. I have seen too many others with the same look in their eyes, as another week of 'just getting by' stretches out ahead, instead of a week of life to be lived to the full.

Some people live a life of relative happiness among all the monotonous routines. They settle for a fraction of what could be: a life so much better, fuller, and more rewarding. Other people feel a sense of restlessness. They remember the dreams they once had. They remember what it was to feel like they could do anything with this short life. It reaches a point when they can take it no more, they threaten to make changes, to jack it all in and to start again. They long to break free of a mundane life that feels so safe, normal, boring, draining. They are going to do something, do more, anything to break this mould. But then they look at those around them, or take advice from those who appear to be doing well, to be making it through. Those who seem on the face of it to be happy and successful. Some do still make the decision to change, to do what makes them feel more alive. Others start thinking about what is at stake. The car, the house, the career. Too much to lose. They settle back into the safety of the half-life they have been leading. They sleep on it. The alarm rings, and the snooze button is hit. They lie a while trying to find some motivation. Legs first, then sit up slowly. Stand up and start the shuffle once again. The shuffle along the path of normality, mapped out ahead by the hedges of expectation.

Where does all the youthful wildness go? How do we become so tamed, so fenced in, when in reality Christ has set us free. Yet we find ourselves in line, plodding along with so many others. Dreams put on the shelf, boxed up and stored away as we do what is expected of us by the society that surrounds us. A tamed life is led as we spend our energy doing what is viewed as normal by a world from which we should be set apart. These things we do to fit in become habit and we can end up bumbling along not really thinking about the real issues - not really thinking about anything until, with our energy drained, we recognise the emptiness of it all.

What if we were to make changes? What if we were to awaken the dreams again? What if we were to break free from the monotony and start running rather than shuffling? Start running and shake up the orderly line. And if we start to live within the hedges of expectation, why not crash on through, jump over, do anything to break free from their confines. Run into wild new realms. Enjoy the excitement and adventure of new terrain ahead. Revel in the thrill of crossing new boundaries, rise above the constraints. Awaken the dreams again and live the unique life that is set before you! It is time to enjoy the freedom that has been bought for us. It is time to free ourselves from norms and expectations. It is time to rise above the blurry half-life and consider how we are being shaped and suppressed. It is time to get to a place where we can see life from a fresh perspective. We need to lift our heads and recognise the empty habits of everyday life so that we can transcend or overcome all the norms and expectations that have ensnared us.

Squares, boxes, flat surfaces and straight lines meet the eye and mind at every turn. Boxes restrain, squares restrict.

Smoothness, regularity, right-angles. I wake and look around a box-like room. In the square mirror I see myself reflected in a box. From behind the windows I see the world in a frame. Out of the door and along the parallel-lines of the pavements' edges. Into a car and I gaze out at the world through more windows. Houses like boxes line the smooth road edges. Televisions flicker in the glowing windows: square plastic boxes with their moving pictures. Into the office cubicle and in front of a computer screen. Everything is so ordered and predictable. If this was my day, every day, if this was all I could see it would be awful. My mind would be more confined than ever by straight-line thinking, limiting logic and restricting reason. My mind in a box would be less open to possibility and diversity and less sensitive to the Spirit.

But this is not all there is. Office work done, now I head out for a short walk through nearby woodland. This whole place is ordered too, held in a most delicate balance. Nowhere though do I see straight lines or boxes or blandness. I follow a burn as it meanders from its source. I step from boulder to boulder. Hundreds, thousands of boulders and no two alike. I brush past pines and broad leaves: Oak, Ash, Beech and Birch. Millions of needles, millions of leaves. No two the same. Insects, birds, animals. Diversity, beauty, freedom. Hills all around, their edges curving. Sky that goes on forever. Scale beyond understanding. Infinity cannot be contained in any box. My usual thought patterns are challenged. My logical ways are altered. My desire for predictability and safety are overwhelmed by intrigue and wonder. Routine is exposed. These are more than simple steps into a wild place that I have taken. These are steps toward a different way of thinking, a different way of living, so I will just keep walking and praying, waiting and praising.

The great nature versus nurture debate! Scientists and psychologists have studied, theorised, debated and puzzled over it for a considerable time. Are we genetically determined from the outset, or do we learn as we live? Are we born pre-programmed to act and react in a certain way, governed by the genetic code that has shaped us? Or do we adapt and learn from those around us and our experiences as life unfolds before us? Some argue that it is genetics that determine who we are. Others say it is socialisation, the process of learning and being shaped by the world around us. The majority acknowledge that it is a bit of both.

As Christians, we know that God shapes us and has a perfect plan for our lives. He knit us together in the womb. He used the DNA of our parents in forming us. The same way that He used some of our grandparents in forming our parents, and some of our great-grandparents to form our grandparents and so on throughout our ancestry. We all show some resemblance to our parents, be it in physical appearance or character traits. But out of the womb God continues to shapes us in other ways. Without delving too deep into the issue of predetermination, we can see that we also learn from people, places, situations and experiences. Only God can know the infinite complexities involved in our formation and ongoing development. God knows us better than we know ourselves and loves us more than we can ever fully understand. He had our life planned before time began. He has created us and shaped us, to some extent, through our parents, but He has also created us with the ability to learn and adapt.

I know that this is a very brief summary of a complex scientific and theological argument. Whole books have been written on the subject. Very thick books with very small font and very big words! Socialisation is recognised by the majority as having a hand in human development. It is the way we learn from each other and from the world around us. Whether this is good or bad depends on how we allow it to shape us.

In some ways the effects of the socialisation process are clear to see, while at other times they are so engrained that the effect is almost impossible to perceive. I think of driving as one of the obvious examples. When I am driving on a quiet road, with no other cars around, I still find myself using the indicators. It is the rules and norms that have been instilled in me since I first learned to drive and have become habit. Another example is the routine and ritual of eating -

particularly eating in a restaurant or other social setting. Conversations may be of current affairs, films, music, work, and the daily things of life, but not with full mouths. Food is cleared from the side of the mouth with a polite dab of a napkin. Knife and fork are held in a particular way. They even signify when we are finished (hopefully not first...or last) when they are laid side by side across the plate. We might have a starter, usually savoury, with the occasional exception. This will be followed by the main course of savoury food. Some red wine or white, depending on the food. And to top it all off, dessert. And maybe a coffee after that. Different utensils are provided for each course despite the fact they will be used for placing food in the same mouth. We feel full half way through the main course but continue eating and order a dessert anyway! We expect salt and pepper to be on the table. In this country we try not to belch though it is a natural part of digestion. Why? Because it is all socially accepted and expected, because it is normal!

At last, a sheltered hollow. Steep banks of snow dropping to a flat area below. Rucksacks are swung from shoulders and dumped on the frozen ground. We sit back and feel the soft snow shape itself around us to form a comfy seat. Our gloves are kept on to protect against the cold. We fumble with the zips and clips and buckles. Little is said. I'm thinking about the food in my pack, about to be relished. I'm sure my friend David is thinking about his own. It is great to share the wild hill experience with someone else who looks around and revels in seeing it as God's wild winter creation, someone else who shares the same beliefs and same enjoyment of travels through creation.

We have been hungry for a while now but this shelter was hard to find. At last the food is extracted from our packs. Bread is torn off in ragged chunks and stuffed in our mouths with gloved hands. It is held tight and eaten quickly before the wind whips it away. Even in this relatively sheltered hollow, the wind blows and snow-flurries whirl about us. Coffee is slurped noisily, swallowed before it can cool so that its warmth is felt inside. Water is gulped. The same cup is shared. The same knife is used for savoury and sweet. We eat for energy; we drink for hydration and heat. Our eating and drinking is brought back to basics and it tastes fantastic! Even this cheap instant coffee that has lain in the flask for hours far surpasses the taste of an extortionate Latte-to-go!

With full mouths our chat continues. Life, death, what comes next, our surrounding environment, where it came from, where we came from, why we are here, all the usual talk of wild places. And between the talk, silence. A most comfortable silence. It seems the most natural thing to sit together in silence, looking out over the white world spread before us, each lost in our own thoughts. There is no such thing as an awkward silence, or bad table manners out here!

Of course table manners or rules of the road are needed and are in place for good reason, but they do highlight some of the more obvious examples of a deeper process. A deeper process that must be examined. It is certainly a positive thing to ask ourselves why we do things or why we act or react in a certain way. We are in a position to ask ourselves if there is a better way. Why, if we have not been living life to the full, have we allowed it to be like that for so long? What if the way the world shapes us through socialisation is not passive, but aggressive? Looking at the process of socialisation in this way can shed light on how powerful a tool it could be if used by Satan to keep us as 'normal', or in a state where we do not really think about the deeper issues. What if this process of socialisation was used to hold us in a life of mediocrity and apathy? Surely it would require some opposing action. Life is too short for us to question everything, but it is vital to take stock regularly and to examine what it is that is guiding and directing us and shaping our life.

The problem is that for many of us we simply conform to the shaping, moulding effects of the world around us. We acknowledge God while at the same time going along just the same as everyone else. Surely those living in light of eternity should be obviously different in word, action and lifestyle, from those living with the mentality that the here and now is all there is. Right at the start of Romans Paul introduces himself as 'an apostle... set apart for the gospel of God'. Later in the first chapter he sums up what has been happening in society at that time –

> 'For although they knew God, they neither glorified him as God nor gave thanks to him, but their thinking became futile and their foolish hearts were darkened. Although they claimed to be wise, they became fools and exchanged the glory of the immortal God for images made to look like mortal man and birds and animals and reptiles'
> (Romans 1:21-23)

Times have changed in some ways but Paul's words remain as relevant to this age as to the time they were written. Many still claim to know God yet live a lifestyle that does nothing to glorify Him. They are caught up in the mentality that places utmost importance on the here and now and they give little thought to eternal matters. It is futile thinking that leads to a high value being placed on things that are immediate and short-term. Fleeting pleasures become our gods, at the expense of deeper, lasting joy. Worship is reserved for anything that offers short-term enjoyment in a shallow life. This futile thinking is prevalent in the society around us. It influences what is perceived as a normal way to live and it fosters expectations in relation to this normality. Despite eternity stretching out before us, many of us conform. We spectacularly fail to be apostles set apart.

Grey, grey, grey. Grey rock before and behind me. Grey rock below and beside me. Grey rock merging into grey skies. Grey cloud that blocks any view from this long, high ridge. This has been my world for hours now. I wander through it alone. I enjoy its simplicity and the contrast it provides to the complexities of society that I have left behind for the day. I have stopped, I don't know why and I don't remember consciously deciding to - I just have. It is another of those moments when the subconscious, or something else takes over, and my body responds to its commands rather than the usual conscious thought processes. Why here I wonder? All is still grey. But the grey to my right, to the north, is changing, softening, lightening, and now it's gone! With the drama and suddenness of a veil being whisked off some new exhibit, the curtain of grey cloud is gone. Before me stretches the finest exhibit I have ever seen. The mountain slope plunges down, down, down before me to meet the southern edge of a vast moor. It is a vast watery trackless wilderness, stretching out in all directions. And onto its numerous lochs pours a wide shaft of brilliantly intense sunlight. The lochs respond by glowing silver. Suddenly the dark moorland is spattered by irregular pools of vibrant liquid silver. Now it is gone again. The grey curtain has been drawn across once again.

I am applauding! I am actually applauding. Here, a few thousand feet up, alone and I am applauding. I have been speaking out loud as well, my voice joining with the wind. Although it is more noises of wonder than actual words. I start to walk again with a grin spread across my face. A huge grin that would stay in place for the remainder of this fine grey day.

Things done because they are expected or because they are the norm are a danger in any area of our life – even our times spent with God. Do you ever sing hymns or songs to Him without much consideration given to the words? During the church service do you act in the same way as those around you, standing when they stand, clapping if they clap, even dancing if they dance? Is it an expression of a heart of worship, or a desire not to stand out from the crowd? Does the way you pray or worship change when other people are around? Would you be surprised if the order of hymns and prayers, or the time allocated for worship on a Sunday morning service changed? Would it affect your worship? Do you sit in the same seat or pew every week? Do you expect an organ to accompany the songs, or a full rock band to back every word? Would you be surprised if one week it was different? Would you be offended? Is your own time of worship governed by routine? Do you do things out of habit? Is the way you worship in a group setting predictable? Do you ever find yourself singing about the overwhelming love of God while your mind is on something else entirely? Surely it is better to do something different. It is far better to shake yourself out of empty habit.

Our worship is a reflection of the state of our life "For where your treasure is, there your heart will be also." (Matthew 6:21) What if breaking free from habits sets us free to worship and live more fully? Vibrant and varied worship, as people offer themselves to God, fully and genuinely and driven by gratitude for His grace and mercy. Vibrant and varied worship as people are filled with awe at His majesty and splendour, and overwhelmed with appreciation for what He has done for each one of us. Vibrant and varied lives, as people do what God has called them to do. No longer would people be forced into moulds or do things just because they are perceived as normal. People could be set free from mundane routine because they are following God, and their life would be a wild unpredictable adventure like the lives of the disciples. We *should* be different, as we have been created utterly unique. Every word, every action, every move absolutely genuine, compelled and driven by a deep desire to continually walk with God and glorify Him with our lives. And there must be balance. Difference for the sake of being different is just as empty as unthinking habits built around the status quo. It has to be Spirit-led, God-centred and glorifying Jesus. If it is those things then worship will be radical, powerful, unpredictable and wonderful - as will life.

With just a single touch from Jesus we can be transformed. Think of the disciples, Peter, Andrew, James and John. Jesus walked past the boats they were fishing from and said simply: "Come follow me and I will make you fishers of men." (Matthew 4:19) Now these were men with social expectations similar to those many of us face. They were there on the lake working. Work was expected of them. A catch was expected from them. Working and making a living was a daily expectation, as it is for any of us. These expectations did not matter when Jesus spoke to them. He called them, and they responded instantly. Their response was beyond any 'normal' expectation. Verse 20 tells us that: 'At once they (Peter and Andrew) left their nets and followed Him.' Verse 22 tells us that: 'Immediately they (James and John) left the boat and their father and followed Him.' Boats were left on the shore and nets left un-mended. They left their old life and became men who would go down in history as the first followers of Christ, the first of millions that would follow Him.

For the Israelites it took forty years of wandering in the desert to throw off the influences of the society they had been enslaved in. In the wild place they were physically cut off from the bondage of Egyptian culture they had lived under for so long. Many times we read of their grumbling when faced with wilderness hardships. At one point, when bored eating the manna God was providing, they were actually considering that they would be better off forfeiting their freedom so they could go back to Egyptian food! A whole generation had to pass away in the desert, in that culturally-neutral ground, so that the whole nation with God at their head could enter the Promised Land. The old routines, norms, expectations and habits were stripped away and left in the desert so that the whole nation would be God centred and radically different from the one that had left Egyptian slavery.

We can all benefit from freeing ourselves from the restraints on our lives. Muir, in 'The Mountains of California', writes about the difference between a wild meadow and a well-kept lawn:

> "...these wild lawns, with all their exquisite fineness, have no trace of that painful, licked, snipped, repressed appearance that pleasure ground lawns are apt to have.... they respond to the touch of every breeze, rejoicing in pure wildness, blooming and fruiting in the vital light".
>
> (John Muir, 'The Mountains of California')

This description can be seen as a metaphor for socialisation, which is like the shears and the mower, keeping us neat, uniform and straight, and in being so shaped we lose the ability to feel the touch of the breeze of the Spirit. We fail to live under the vital light of God and in doing so we no longer produce fruit. Through spending time with God we are set free to be wild, to follow God's lead, to learn from Him. It takes a lot of work and effort to keep gardens looking good and in order. Leave them alone for even a week or two and the weeds start rising, the grass starts looking clumpy and too long. Neighbours look over the fence and shake their heads! When we fail to adhere to the norms and expectations just for the sake of being different, it can be a bit like that. We start to seem a bit ragged, a bit out of order, in need of some work. But when we genuinely consider what expectations have been keeping us licked, snipped and suppressed and what habits have been keeping us dulled, then things can positively change. When we give ourselves fully to God, in a way that reveals what restraints have been weighing us down, then we can become wild in the most positive sense. Like a high mountain meadow that far surpasses the beauty of any garden. Like a forest with layers of detail, all in harmony. Like a river pouring down cascades and plunging unstoppable into deep pools. Our whole life will be diverse, but balanced. Dreams will be dreamt again and and then lived out. Energy will be spent on things that really matter. Life will be vibrant and varied. It will glorify God who is shaping us.

Even here among the trees, that so effectively dampen sound, the noise is growing. It is a constant roar emanating from some distant point, mingled with the more immediate but delicate patter of raindrops on leaves. I near the forest edge and the patter of the drops are drowned out by the roar of the flowing rapids. Tree cover gone, I look up the slope to my right. Up to the point where the soft irregular carpet of green meets with smooth dark concrete of dam wall that rises to tower above me. Up it rises almost vertically to meet with the curving top hundreds of feet above. It curves as though the volume of water behind is causing it to bulge under the force of its constant weight.

Standing here dwarfed by the wall, I imagine it being made of glass, and that I can stare along the valley. I imagine the mountain slopes sweeping down to meet in a v-shape at the bottom. And down it's course would flow the river as it used to be, before the building of the great dam. Over cascades and into deep pools, trees growing from the banks, heather slopes rising above. I wonder do the trees still stand, leafless now, in the dark depths of the reservoirs floor? I wonder do fish now swim among the branches where once the birds flitted and sang?

My gaze sweeps up the smooth concrete again to where the water is flowing. It flows out and plunges in a white column and down onto the original rock-strewn riverbed. The white column dwarfs the silver pipes that normally carry away the water. So much water pours into the reservoir above that these pipes cannot cope and so the floodgates have been opened. The floodgates are flung wide and water rushes unstoppable down its original course. Spray rises from where it smashes against unmoving rocks. Sound rises with it. A sense of power is felt in the soft mist that emanates from the force of unstoppable water hitting immovable rock. Leaves sway as the spray drenches them. Rocks are washed clean. The dams of fallen leaves and branches are swept away like paper in a storm. Their stagnating water is replaced with the fresh water that flows so forcefully.

I look down the valley and stare at this ribbon of white flowing powerfully towards the sea. The whole valley is changed. This white force is the focal-point. This energy that cannot be harnessed, flowing once again over the course that was set for it. And it will keep flowing, as long as the rain keeps falling. As long as vast quantities of water keep flowing into the reservoir above, the floodgates will remain open and no hindrance will stand in the rivers way.

'A Call For All' (top)
'How Wild A Wilderness?' (bottom)

'At Risk Without Risk' (top)
'See, Hear, Smell, Taste, Feel...Know' (bottom)

'Between A rock And A Momentarily Hard Place' (top)
'Mountains Into Molehills' (bottom)

'Self-Sufficient Dependency' (top)
'Beyond The Trees' (bottom)

£ $ € ¥
(Freedom From Materialism)

We buy, we sell. Sales rise, sales fall. Salaries increase, profits increase. Interest rates go up, inflation keeps rising. Oil prices rise, oil prices sink. Money comes in, money goes out. We want more for less. We want to give less and gain more. Stock markets secure, stock markets collapse. Currency used less, credit cards used more. Numbers going up, numbers going down. More debts accumulated. House prices still rising. Cost of living still rising. Pension schemes failing. Endowment policies falling short. New work sought. Promotions chased. More overtime required. Bills come in. More bills come in. Tax paid. More tax paid. Standing orders and direct debits. More money in, more money out. We want, we need. We call wants 'needs'. We buy more. We need more, we need, we need, we want.

> "No one can serve two masters. Either he will hate one and love the other, or he will be devoted to one and despise the other. You cannot serve both God and money."
>
> (Jesus Christ, Matthew 6:24)

Who are you serving?

We live in a world that revolves around money and materialism. The whole fabric of society seems to be stitched together with the threads of finance and commerce. Everywhere we look we see its influence. Watch the satellite news channels and often while the daily disasters are reported, the latest stocks and shares and market figures are revealed at the bottom of the screen. We watch footage of the latest terrorist atrocity, the latest report on global warming, the latest political row, the latest famine, plane crash, murder, war, or any other disaster and there at the bottom of the screen is the financial index and how it has been impacted.

How do we function in this materialistic world? I remember reading a report called the 'identity parade'. In the parade, wealth was attributed to height. For example, someone on an average income would be allocated a height of perhaps six feet. Those on benefits stood only inches tall. More shocking were those at the other end of the spectrum. Their heights were not measured in feet and inches but in miles, revealing the vast inequality in wealth distribution. To what extent do we participate in this parade? Do we strive too hard to gain some financial 'height'? How strong is our desire to be rich? What would we sacrifice to achieve earthly riches? Are we even aware that when we pursue wealth, we quickly switch our masters?

In the gospels we read that Peter, accompanying Jesus to Capernaum, arrived and did not have the money required by the local tax collectors. Jesus told Peter to go and cast a line into the lake. Peter did as instructed, caught a fish, and from its mouth took a coin of enough value to cover his and Jesus' tax. Jesus could have simply spoken authoritatively and the demanded tax would have been waived. Or He could have produced it from a fold in His robes, or changed a stone into a coin. But why from a fish's mouth? It seems that Jesus was making a different point. I wonder did Peter smile as he pulled the coin from the fish's mouth. I wonder did he look around at all the other fishermen on the lake trying to make enough money to live comfortably in a society that was possibly no less financially oriented than our own. I wonder did he realise the futility of worrying about money and wealth? Was it then that he realised that God who so splendidly clothes the flowers of the fields and provides for the birds, would also provide for him? I wonder did Peter walk back to pay the taxes, less ensnared by financial traps than ever before?

Each and every one of us owes Jesus more than we could ever pay, for He gave His life for all of us. Think of a small Scottish island with its fifty inhabitants and the phenomenal collective debt they owe! Now think of a small country, like Ireland with its several-million inhabitants. Their debt is immeasurable. If all material wealth was collected and all the money in that nation added together, if every credit card was used, every account emptied, every house offered, every car given, still the debt owed to Jesus would be no closer to being paid. The accumulative wealth of every nation is nothing compared to what He has given. He gave His all so that we may live, yet when the Capernaum tax was demanded, Jesus paid it. He demonstrated that we can live in a money orientated society yet remain above it, free from its snares and traps. We should work, we should pay taxes and we can earn money. But like Jesus, and because of Him, we should remain free from the traps, free from the grip money can have on us. We should be aware of the wrong attitudes humorously highlighted by the coin from the fish's mouth. We should be free from the desires to be rich - we are already rich. God provides for all we need. What does the story of the coin from the fish's mouth highlight to you? Do you need to trust God more? Do you need to bring the whole area of finance before Him and stop struggling and striving to make it on your own? Do you need to rethink some of your priorities? Do you need to hold onto things more lightly? Do you need to shake off the hold money has on you? Do you need to trust more in God's resources and provision?

What an empty pursuit it is, this chasing of material and financial wealth. We could spend a huge chunk of our life working in a job that we do not enjoy, but one that brings in plenty of money. Suddenly we find that we are too old or too sick to enjoy spending the money we worked so hard for and then we spend the rest of our life looking back on all the things we wish we had done. The ways we wished we had lived. The people we should have made more time for, the important things we overlooked, and the places we should have visited. Right now you can decide not to make that mistake. We come into the world with nothing and leave it with nothing as Paul reminds us in 1 Timothy 6:7. It is wealth of a different sort that we should pursue: lasting wealth, treasures in heaven.

It is our attitudes we have to watch and what we place value on that matters. What do we put our hope in? What do we strive for or make our idol? We have an abundant God so we should not live a meagre life, but that cannot be used as an excuse to justify the pursuit of riches. And what we have, we must hold onto lightly and we must tithe what we have. As we can see from the word of God, it is a principle He takes very seriously:

> "'Return to me, and I will return to you,' says the Lord Almighty. But you ask, "How are we to return? Will a man rob God?" Yet you rob me. But you ask, "How do we rob you?" "In tithes and offerings you are under a curse - the whole nation of you - because you are robbing me. Bring the whole tithe into the storehouse, that there may be food in my house. Test me in this," says the Lord Almighty, "and see if I will not throw open the floodgates of heaven and pour out so much blessing that you will not have room enough for it."
>
> (Malachi 3:7-10)

We must do what God leads us to do, and trust that He will provide. And He does provide.

> "Which of you, if his son asks for bread, will give him a stone? Or if he asks for a fish, will give him a

snake? If you, then, though you are evil, know how
to give good gifts to your children, how much more
will your Father in heaven give good gifts to those
who ask him!"

(Matthew 7:9-11)

God sent His son to die for us. God has given us the
greatest gift, the gift of life. God is a God of abundant blessing;
He loves to give us the desires of our hearts. He knows the
desires of our heart more than we know them ourselves. He
knows what will bring us the joy we seek. God knows what
will bring us long term blessing but our attitudes must be
right. The Israelites entered a land 'flowing with milk and
honey'. They entered a land of abundant blessing. They could
only enjoy this blessing once wrong attitudes had been dealt
with. They followed God and learned that He would provide
on a daily basis. Only then did they receive abundantly. And
if the material things were stripped away again, it would
not matter, for God would still be with them. They would
still be rich beyond measure.

When we have God in our lives we have all we need.
The pursuit of riches is absurd because true contentment
or true happiness cannot be bought. God gives these things
freely when we see Him, as He desires us to see Him - as our
Father. And when our response is that we happily follow
His ways, then the rewards we experience go way beyond
anything that can be purchased. We can realise more fully
that the source of all happiness and lasting joy does not come
from any material wealth. We can be set free to live simply,
to live without the constant desire to pursue riches. We can
fully appreciate what we have and know that even if those
things were taken away, we would still be rich.

It is a positively freeing experience when the source
of all joy, true contentment and happiness, is realised
more fully. I remember clearly being impacted with this
realisation on a camping trip with my father. We looked
out over stunning mountain scenery. We slept in the most
basic of shelters; we ate simple meals and drank from a
little stream of the clearest, most refreshing water. There

was no telephone, television, radio or any other distraction. We just enjoyed chatting and laughing together in a place of simplicity, surrounded by silence and filled with peace. We were absolutely content lying back on the rugged grasses and looking out across the mountains. It was not the view over wild creation that brought the contentment; it was much more. It was an awareness of the awesomeness of our Creator God. It was looking around and seeing His character revealed. It was looking around at the beauty of the natural scene in the knowledge that we are saved and before us lies an eternity of wonders. Wonders of which the surrounding beauty at our campsite was just the merest hint. While the kettle boiled over a methylated spirit flame, our eyes roamed the cliffs and lochs, and the surrounding summits. At that moment neither of us would have swapped our site for a room in the worlds most luxurious hotel.

If we allow God to give us a new perspective we can, like Paul, be 'apostles set apart.' We will shine. In a mad, money centred world, a healthy God-given perspective on material wealth will have us shining like lamps on stands. Living in the knowledge that God is our only hope, the only place we turn to for the satisfaction of our needs, will set us free from the yoke of financial slavery and worry. We will be free so that we can free others. We just need to keep asking ourselves a question -Who am I serving?

The rain stops and almost immediately a lark's song rings out from high above. With a flutter of brown wings, another rises almost vertically and more song fills the air. Higher and higher until it is just a speck and still its freedom-song is heard across the hillscape. Singing as only the free can sing. Rising as only the unburdened can rise. At my feet an orchid grows among the grasses. Its rich-green leaves spattered with dark spots stand out clearly against the lighter-green grasses. From the foliage a stem stands proud, supporting a most delicate and detailed flower. Water glistens on the rich-green robe of leaves. The detailed and colourful flower-crown sways elegantly in the wind. On across the heather and grasses I wander. I carry nothing, in the knowledge that

I have all I need. I walk on feeling incredibly rich.

> "Come ... come, all who need rest and light, come,
> all who are bending and breaking over with work,
> leave your profits and losses and metallic dividends
> and come...."
> (John Muir, 'My first Summer in Sierra')

John Muir seems to have caught the very heart of God in these words. God is speaking to all His people. His desire is clear through His Word. He is gently calling us to Him. He is calling us to leave our worries and striving behind. He is calling us out of the busyness and emptiness of the rat race. He is calling us to come to Him and find rest and contentment. He is calling us to meet with Him and to listen as He speaks words of love. He is calling us to live in the freeing light of life eternal. The God of all creation speaks words of truth to us. Why would we serve anyone or anything else?

A Place To Ponder
(Freedom From Distractions)

'There is something in walking that stirs and quickens
my ideas... the sight of the country, the succession
of agreeable views, the open air, the big appetite,
the good health I win by walking ... the absence
of everything that makes me feel my dependence,
everything that reminds me of my situation, all this
loosens my soul.'
> (Jean Jacques Rousseau, 'Confessions')

Infinity is a subject we just can't fully grasp. We try, but
it is like plunging our hands into the ocean, clenching
our fists and then opening them up to realise that we
have caught so little. Similarly, the love of God - do we
really understand it? Do we realise how much escapes us,
how little we have grasped? Do we look at the water pulled
from the ocean and see that it has trickled out between
our fingers? Can we really grasp the fact that eternal life
stretches out before us? What a meagre little pool of water
is left in the palm of our hand compared to the vast volume

that remains in the sea! Vastness, infinity, eternity, the love of God, the splendour of God, the power of God. His majesty, His grace, and Heaven, our eternal home. With these finite minds we cannot fully understand these subjects, yet that does not mean we shouldn't think about them. We need to think about the bigger issues. We need to take our focus off all the immediacy and short-term things that surround us on a daily basis. We need to find a time and a place in our busy life for thinking. A place of silence and stillness, a place to wait on God, a place to have our minds renewed. It is good to think. We grasp so little, yet the glimmer we get is enough. It is enough to shape us, to fill us with hope, to have us live with a different perspective. Yes, it is positive to wrestle with such questions. It is releasing and freeing.

Where do you go to think?

"A Cinquecento... the smallest car on the road... are you joking?" asks Simon. I respond to his shocked voice by reminding him that it was he who had told me to hire the cheapest car I could for our weekend away. At the same time I did agree that a little more money might have been worth it for the extra space for the round trip of a few hundred miles. Four of us with full weekend packs in the smallest roadworthy car was perhaps slightly ambitious!

Simon quickly planted himself in the driver's seat, stating that for safety reasons he would need plenty of leg room, thus his seat could go no further forward! Andrew claimed the passenger seat suggesting that he could squeeze his backpack in beside him. The boot could only take one rucksack so Ross and I were squeezed into the back seat along with the other two. The logic behind this being that physically Ross was the smallest and my place in the back was secured as punishment for booking the car. At least it was warm inside, as outside the temperature remained in the minus figures even during the daylight hours. Despite the risk of ice, particularly on the long single-track road winding through the remote glen, Simon had us there in good time. Even with the weight on board he managed to leave the road on at least two occasions over the hump backed bridges, or 'ju-hump back' bridges as he delightedly renamed them.

After struggling stiffly from the cramped confines of the car and gradually standing up straight, the beauty of the surrounding scene struck us with full force. Never before had the mountain wilderness seemed so vast! The car was left at the road-end car park and off we set on another journey and adventure together. We came to a stile and squeezed through, Ross commenting that the car would probably have fitted! All around us branches hung low, laden in a thick coat of pure-white frost. The gravel track underfoot was as solid as tar; the water had solidified and joined each piece of gravel together into a continuous mat. The loch glimmered, reflecting the blue sky above and the white mountains on either side. Stretching up the slope beside us was a forest of beautifully knurled and twisted pines (true Scots Pine) with broken branches and red upper trunks. This forest gave an ancient feel to the beauty of the glen, and a strange but pleasant humbling feeling. Purity, freshness, reviving, rejuvenating – there are a lack of words to describe this frozen walk that took us further and further from the road-end car park with its stationary tiny red car. Further and further our steps carried us into an unspoilt wilderness where every glance revealed views that pointed to something beyond our grasp. Space, time, holiness, power, and glory, all things beyond our ability to fathom but all things that over the next few days we would find ourselves pondering. This is the effect of wild creation.

Of course in this wild setting we would inevitably find ourselves ill-equipped and out of our depth on snow-covered and ice-crusted slopes. At one point near the summit of one of the many high peaks the wind had cleared away the soft snow leaving a huge sheet of blue-black ice as hard as the rock it covered. We edged our way slowly up using any little edge we could find as grip. On the final steeper section we ended up using knives and forks to chip out little edges so that we could continue on our route!

Back in the safety of the valley after the world of wind

and ice above, we came across an empty wood shack. This we
unanimously decided would serve as our home for the night.
Outside we gathered some wood and soon had a fire roaring.
After a good meal we got in our sleeping bags and lay as
close to the fire as we dared. Before heading into the shack
we lay watching the flames die down to a softly glowing bed
of embers, and as they did a mass of stars were revealed
stretching out into the infinity above. It was so clear that
they genuinely twinkled, set against their backdrop of black
space. There were no lights for miles around and even the
moon was the thinnest of slivers. The steep snow covered
slopes rose all around, looking soft and inviting in this
gentlest of lights. The sweep of those slopes made us feel
somehow cosy lying there on the valley floor. And yet lying
there around the fading glow of the embers and staring at
infinity we all shared a heightened awareness of just how
small we felt and how incredibly short our time here on
earth is. The discussions were of infinity, eternal life, God,
creation, and death. Despite me being the only committed
Christian there at the time this talk seemed as natural as the
setting around us. I spoke as freely about my faith as I ever
had to anyone and it felt completely natural. Praising God
and speaking about Him, His eternal love and divine nature,
His love for us, His incredible creation – these topics seemed
the only things worth opening our mouths for. For someone
who does not know God, the subject of heaven, eternal life,
the sacrifice of Jesus and faith, can seem forced, un-natural,
challenging or irrelevant. This results in our feeling that it
is an uphill struggle to share what we believe! Yet out there
under the multitude of stars and surrounding mountains it
was either this or silence. Any other conversation seemed
futile and shallow. All the usual trivial talk seemed so out
of place and awkward. All around us that winter night it
seemed creation was calling out in a language understood
by all:

> 'The heavens declare the glory of God; the skies
> proclaim the works of his hands. Day after day they
> pour forth speech; night after night they display

knowledge. There is no speech or language where
their voice is not heard. Their voice goes out into all
the earth, their words to the end of the world'

(Psalm 19:1-4).

I have sat in similar situations with fellow believers and
pondered the wonders of creation. The infinite and eternal
nature of God and the deep mystery that surrounds Him. I
have heard prophecy, prayer and praise that goes to deeper
levels, that responds to the depth of God as deep calls out to
deep. I have listened to testimonies of a renewed intimacy
found when people spend time alone with God.   I have
watched tears roll down the faces of believers as they speak
unashamedly of the new revelation of the love their Father
has for them. I have seen lives restored through meeting
with God in green meadows, and beside quiet waters. I have
experienced it myself.

In natural settings I have found myself set free to
wander and my mind responds by dreaming and pondering,
always searching out beyond the here and now. Distractions
are removed and my mind gets drawn upward and outward.
The wilds are an arena of freedom where our minds have
time to ponder. Among society it can be harder to ponder
such things. We get caught up in a society that is based
around immediacy and short-term perspective. Distraction
is everywhere. Technology has provided us with countless
distractions. Television in particular is a major source of
distraction.

The sequence of images caught on film flick across the
screen so fast that they look like a single moving image. It
is a box of illusions and it has a place in almost every home
in the westernised world, available twenty-four hours a day,
seven days a week with numerous channels. Constantly
changing, moving, and feeding the mind, its pace leaves
little time for thinking. We just swallow all that the illusion
feeds us. We drink it all in, most of the time not even aware
that we are doing so. There are plenty of options, and we can
just push a button to change the channel. So many options,

pictures, and layers of sound. Music and voice-overs layered on top of one another, and a whole host of other sounds thrown in for effect. Fast, loud, hyped up and non-stop. All the sex and violence and immorality are just a small part of the problem. The banality of television is just as bad. We sit watching rubbish for the simple reason that it is there. Many people know more about the lives of soap-opera stars than they do about what is happening in the lives of those in their own family and friends. How many people struggle to find time for prayer and praise and reading the scriptures, but at the same time, would not even consider missing their favourite television programmes?

It's the banality of all distractions, not just TV that we must resist. There is nothing wrong with watching a bit of television. There are some great programmes on, and many inspirational films. When our watching becomes excessive or we start watching trash for the sake of having the TV switched on, then it is a problem. Being distracted takes our mind off eternal thoughts and our infinite God and anchors them to the here and now shallowness of the world that surrounds us. It's like a ship tied to the dock, never setting out into the freedom of the open waters with all that space to explore, and height above and depth below. It remains chained to the pier and misses out on doing what it was built to do. How great it is when we refocus on the things of true importance and ignore the shallow distractions around us. "Since, then, you have been raised with Christ, set your hearts on things above, where Christ is seated at the right hand of God. Set your minds on things above, not on earthly things." (Colossians 3:1&2) We have to keep remembering that God wants us to be in the world but not of it. While we live in the world, our hearts and our minds must be set on higher things, heavenly things. That does not mean we completely alienate ourselves from those around us. It is possible to keep our minds on higher things yet remain relevant and effective in the dark world around us. To live in this world without conforming to its patterns we need to have a place where the distractions of our modern age are left well behind. So where can it be? When can it be?

Why not take a day off work to wander through creation as spring arrives and colour is erupting from the warming earth? Would you set aside a day to stroll through wooded valleys and over purple heather hills? Maybe during your lunch hour, wandering through a nearby park where flowers of every shape and colour line the path? Why not try taking your child out in the pushchair or baby carrier, and watch them gaze up at the blue skies beyond the waving leaves. See their eyes close as they descend into peaceful sleep to the gentle sounds of nature? Start them young! Or maybe try taking a different route to work, stopping in the country and looking over fields and forests? What about missing that television programme so that you can spend the time walking along the banks of a river, or sitting beside a still loch? What about taking the dog for a longer walk through fields and along country lanes? (I'm sure the dog would like that idea!) Spend a summer evening walking through the countryside, listening to birds sing their cheerful tunes and insects buzz lazily past. How about sitting on a park bench and watching the autumnal colour of the leaves falling gently through the air to land softly beside you? What about wandering through woods when frost creates new patterns on the bark, when branches droop with the weight of snow, and a white carpet covers the fallen leaves? What about sitting amidst that white stillness with a flask of hot coffee, simply revelling in the silence of the white snowy world around you? What about taking time to watch a sunset, or a sunrise? How about watching as the light of a new day floods into a valley, or the light of a passing day fades away? It is time to decide. It is time to set aside some time and find a place. Do it and allow God to speak to you of His marvellous ways and of His unending love for you. Allow Him to reveal more of what He has is store for you. Allow Him to bring you comfort, to expand your life, to cheer you, to fill you with excitement and satisfaction. Allow Him to be your Father.

> "Sol y Sombra. . . . . . [Sun and Shade]
> The strange, solid light which comes at the fading of day,
> Drawing the shadows from their hiding places,

As it slices through the land.
The journeys end?
No, just a flashing glimpse of eternity,
A moment of unbridled brilliance,
Heaven touching earth, igniting a passion
So deep, so powerful,
I will never be the same again."
                              (Isobel Triay, 'Sol y Sombra')

Can you hear it? Can you hear His call? Can you hear His desire to meet intimately with you? Where is He leading you? What will He reveal to you? What exciting adventure is He calling you into? We need it. We need this time in our daily lives that is set aside and free from distractions. No televisions, no internet, mobile phones and radios switched off. We need a quiet place where we can refocus the mind on things above and away from all the earthly distractions.

Mary sat at Jesus' feet and focused on Him alone, while her sister Martha, we are told in Luke 10:40, "was distracted by all the preparations that had to be made." Martha thought she had it right, she thought she was the one serving Jesus best. She was wrong. Even though her intentions were good, she, like her sister needed to take her sights off her work and simply sit in adoration at the feet of Jesus. The natural world around us, the little corners of wilderness landscape, the vast open moor-lands, sweeping hillsides, forests and shore-lines, all offer physical separation from the usual distractions. There seems something pure and simple about it. No distractions, and all that surrounds seem to point to our Creator. In those places we can sit at His feet in uninterrupted adoration.

Very often time spent alone with God is where the battles of our lives are won. So many times I have tried and failed to do things in my own strength. Finally, I have spent time away from the struggle and brought it before God. In that place the struggle is dealt with. It is the place where I find my direction, my purpose in life, my reason for being. An intimate encounter with God is at once a life changing experience. I think of Jacob and one of the most significant experiences in his life - the dream of a stairway to heaven as described in Genesis 28. At the time he was fleeing the wrath of his brother. Jacob however set aside time to be still amidst the distraction of direct pursuit and the distraction of his family camp. In that place he fell asleep and received the incredible dream and word from God. As is so often the case, God moves in an incredible way in the lives of His followers when they are away from their normal situations and well clear of all distraction. While Jacob had lain down to rest in a quiet nondescript place, upon waking he sees it differently, stating, "How awesome is this place; it is none other than the house of God and the gate of heaven" (Genesis 28:17). Suddenly the site was seen as a place of utmost importance. He had his eyes opened and his focus had been moved from the physical realm to the heavenly realm. The place of stillness, calm and quiet had played an important role in this process. Remote roads, hillsides, mountaintops, caves, fields, forests, riverbanks, beaches – throughout the scriptures there are many places of calm and stillness that God chooses to meet with man.

Moses demonstrates the importance of this uninterrupted time for our battles to be won. As the Israelites walked toward battle in the valleys around Rephidim, near Mount Sinai, Moses was not where a leader would be expected to be: at the head of the army. Exodus 16:10 tells us that while "Joshua fought the Amalekites as Moses had ordered, Moses, Aaron and Hur went to the top of the hill." Standing on top of the hill with his two assistants we read that while Moses had his hands raised to God, the Israelites were winning and when he lowered them the Amalekites were winning. Moses knew where the battle would be won. There was much effort in the valley with Joshua and the men, but the battle was being won on the hilltop. Imagine the distractions if Moses had remained in the valley, the noise, arrows flying past, people shouting orders, people asking Moses for orders. Moses knew to separate himself from all of this. He knew the importance of an uninterrupted encounter with God. His life and the lives of many others depended upon it.

When we get distracted we lose our focus, we take our

eyes off Jesus and the path God has laid before us. Our
compass for following that path is the Holy Spirit and we
need to spend some quiet time just waiting. We live in a
world where everything is speeding up, and we respond by
doing the same. As Foster writes, "Busyness is not of the
devil, busyness is the devil." We need to slow down and stop
and listen, as scripture tells us:

> "Be still before the Lord and wait patiently for him;
> do not fret when men succeed in their ways, when
> they carry out their wicked schemes."
> (Psalm 37:7)
> "Be still and know that I am God; I will be exalted
> among the nations, I will be exalted in the earth."
> (Psalm 46:10)
> "Be still before the Lord all mankind, because he has
> roused himself from his holy dwelling." (Zechariah
> 2:13)
> "The Lord is my shepherd, I shall not be in want.
> He *makes* me lie down in green pastures, he *leads*
> me beside quiet waters, he restores my soul." (Psalm
> 23:1 - 3, emphasis mine)
> "Better a dry crust with peace and quiet than a house
> full of feasting, with strife." (Proverbs 17:1)
> "This is what the Sovereign Lord, the Holy One of
> Israel, says: 'In repentance and rest is your salvation,
> in quietness and trust is your strength." (Isaiah
> 30:15)
> "Then, because so many people were coming and
> going that they did not even have a chance to eat, he
> (Jesus) said to them, 'Come with me by yourselves to
> a quiet place and get some rest.'" (Mark 6:30)

God has made it clear through His word. Jesus has
made it clear through His example - we need to find a place
for peace and quiet in our lives. We need a space to think.
We need somewhere to be still and know the presence of our

Father. We need to lie down in green pastures. We need to wander by still waters. We need to stroll through woodlands where the rustle of the leaves is the only sound. Where the birds flying to and fro is the only movement. We need to take time to look at the skies that so clearly reveal the works of our Father's hands, and display His knowledge so vividly. We need to surround ourselves with the peacefulness of God's creation, away from all the distractions of a fast paced human centric society. We need to set aside time to wait, to simply sit and wait and listen. We need to have our souls restored. We need to hear the whisper of our God. So where and when are you going to do it?

I sit with my back against the sandstone cliff face. The ledge on which I rest is just wide enough so that with my legs outstretched, only my feet dangle over the edge. What a view spreading out before me! The sinking sun that sets fire to the thin slivers of cloud illuminates the vastness of sky out west. Thin slivers of burning, glowing cloud arc elegantly, matching and complimenting the sweeping curve of the hills across the valley. Below, the burn flows along the valley floor that now lies in evening shade. Sunlight still strikes this ledge and floods into the little cave that will be our shelter for the night.

The fire hisses and crackles, tended by my friends David and Jonathan, doing what their biblical namesakes must have done so often. Thankfully no angry Saul is pursuing us up the valley! We discuss our wild environment. We talk about food, about eternity, why we are here and where we are headed. We chat about our inability to fully grasp the now star-strewn blackness that stretches out endlessly above us. We consider how small our fire on the cliff face must seem if viewed from high above... from the sky... the stratosphere... the moon... even from other planets. How tiny we are! Our talk dances from simple chat between good friends to ethereal and cosmic considerations. And between the words is a welcomed silence. Each lost in our own thoughts, our own appreciation, and our own memories. Watching, thinking, feeling. Watching our Father's creation subtly shift from day to night. Thinking about everything, inspired by the natural landscape around us, and feeling the deep joy that comes from being silent in God's presence.

Mountains Into Molehills

(Freedom To Gain Perspective)

There he lies in the bottom of the dry well. Only bruises cover his otherwise naked body. In the murky light of the well he lies, stripped of all he once had – and by his own brothers! Brothers so filled with jealousy that they sit above the well plotting to kill him. In the cool dark he listens as their voices carry down to the echoey depths. He listens as they decide not to kill him, but to sell him as a slave instead. He listens as they begin to barter. He listens as his life is traded for twenty pieces of silver. Joseph the dreamer, loved by his father, hated by his brothers, sold as a slave.

What problems are you facing?

Side by side, step-by-step, they walk along the track. For Ruth, with tear-stained cheeks, there is a path of uncertainty stretching out before her. For Naomi there is only emptiness. Emptiness in front and emptiness inside. Too empty even for tears. Behind both of them are the broken remnants of the life they had known and the grief for those they had loved and lost. For Ruth it is the death of her husband, now each step carries her away from her homeland, her family, her friends, and her people. Before her lies the homeland of her mother-in-law, whose side she refuses to leave. Naomi leaves behind her dead husband and two dead sons. Now each step takes her back to her homeland empty. Utterly empty. Step by step these two women walk along the empty path.

What hardships have you experienced in the past and what lies ahead?

There he is in the gloomy corner of the cave, the prophet Elijah, his cloak pulled around him. There he is cowering in the corner, dejected and so discouraged that he longs for God to take his life. He wills it all to be over. This prophet who had challenged kings, who had received the food provided by God, carried to him by the ravens. This prophet who had stood and faithfully declared that only the God of Israel was all-powerful. There he sits, hiding away in a dank cave. Discouraged and frightened. There he hides as the wind batters his shelter. A wind so powerful that it shakes the mountain in which he hides. Then an earthquake causes the whole land to tremble followed by a raging fire. Still the prophet hides away.

Are you feeling discouraged?

There he sits among the ashes. Sitting among the charred remains of that which was once so good, that which he had worked hard for. There Job sits having lost almost everything. All his livestock stolen or killed, and most of his servants with them. His sons and daughters crushed to death by the house collapsing around them as the wind laid it flat. All of them dead. All of his children that he had loved so dearly. There he sits in agony, covered from the top of his head to the soles of his feet in festering sores. Sores that peel and turn black - as black as the scorched earth upon which he sits. His body is wasting away. Fever wrecks him. Nightmares mean that even in sleep he can find no relief. Mental and physical pain. Pain day and night for Job the servant of God.

Do you feel that you have lost the things you hold dear?

Darkness. Absolute darkness to the extent that it matters not if this mans eyes are open or closed. All around him is a rubbery softness. He can feel it under him, above him, surrounding him. He feels it with his hands as he braces himself against the constant lolling movement. Nothing solid in this cramped compartment. And the stench that surrounds him, a putrid acrid smell unlike anything ever smelt before. Every breath causes him to taste it, causes him to wretch and gag. No escape from the burning sensation on his skin. His eyes sting. Fear consumes him. The fear that this will be the end. The fear that he will spend his last living hours or days in the dark belly of this great fish. There in the darkness and the stench lies Jonah, regretting his decision to stray from the path that God had laid before him.

Have you lost sight of where you are heading?

There they stand. Persecuted for their faith and the miraculous works they have done in the name of Jesus. There they stand facing the vicious Sanhedrin. The prisoners stand listening as the Pharisees, the elders and teachers and high priests, blinded by pride, arrogance, and religiosity, decide their fate. Side by side, facing imprisonment or death they await their sentence, but they listen as they are set free because the Sanhedrin fear that the sentence of death could start a riot. And so they are freed, but on the condition that they do not speak the name of Jesus again, or preach the good news. Twelve apostles under strict orders not to do the very thing they live to do.

Do you ever feel persecuted for your faith?

There he sits, with his back against the cold prison wall, the chains cutting into his flesh as they secure him to the stone. There he sits, awaiting trial and execution. No cockerel crows now. Peter would not deny the name of his saviour this time. Images of James and John, his friends and fellow apostles, still fresh in his mind. The image of their deaths at the sharp edge of the sword while the Jews watch and cheer excitedly. The same people who will watch and cheer as he is put to death.

Do you feel bound up?

There he kneels in the dusty earth, his face turned toward the sky. Blow after blow felt as stones hurled in ferocious anger crash against his damaged body. Pain flares with each blow, shooting out in all directions from point of impact, so that his whole body seems to consist only of pain. Hard stone splitting flesh and breaking bone. The crack and thud of their impact. Blood dripping onto the dry earth. Seeping away like the life from his body. Blood dripping from wounds. Blood soaking his clothes as Stephen's life is so violently taken from him.

Do you feel that your problems are too much to handle?

Surely for those men and women described above, their problems would overwhelm them. Surely they would be driven to absolute despair? Their problems must have been too great for them to face. Surely their hardships would consume them and destroy them completely?

Not for Joseph the slave. He remained faithful to God, and as a result rose from slave to ruler and his brothers came and bowed before him. The same brothers who had thrown him in the well, plotted to kill him and who sold him as a slave, years later came and bowed at his feet. Joseph, with the wave of a hand, could have ordered that they be put to death. He could have sought revenge for the way they had treated him; he could have given them what they deserved;

he could have done to them what they had done to him. No! Instead Joseph reassures them and provides for their needs. Joseph, through staying close to God, rose above any problem he faced and forgave those who had wronged him.

Even in the most difficult of times and faced with uncertainty, Ruth and Naomi persevered. They would not allow their problems to overwhelm them. Through faithfulness, courage and hard work they became part of a family of great renown. From emptiness God led them into fullness.

And what of Elijah? Did he spend the rest of his days cowering in the dank corner of his cave? Did he stay hidden away through storms and earthquakes and fires until his life passed away just as he had hoped? No! For in the gentle breeze he heard the voice of his loving God. He left the hiding place and came to stand at the mouth of the cave to listen. There he stood and received his instructions from God. In his time of despair he had continued to listen. Through intimacy with God he overcame despair and fear, then strode boldly back toward society to carry out the will of God.

Poor Job! Surely his problems were too much. Surely they would be the end of him. Could any man or woman withstand such hardship? Such were Jobs' problems that his friends sat beside him for seven days, unable to speak, unable to find any words of comfort. But Job continued to trust in God, and God spoke to him. Through His words God reminded Job just how powerful He is and reassured him that He is in control. Job praised God; even in those awful times Job praised Him, knowing that nothing could be done that was not the will of God. Because of his faithfulness, God blessed the latter part of Job's life with more than he had before. He blessed him abundantly with material blessings and a full happy life. Job even lived to see his great grandchildren!

Surely there would be no escape for Jonah. Surely his

time was up. Yet in the stinking darkness of the fish's belly Jonah cried out to God. Jonah realised he was well off the path that God had laid before him and he vowed to make it right. God answered Jonah. God commanded the great fish to vomit Jonah onto dry land, and back onto the path that He had set before him. In his deepest moments of despair Jonah knew that the only place to turn was to God. Jonah went on to deliver the message that God had asked him to take to Nineveh.

What of the twelve apostles, commanded to stop speaking the good news and using the name of Jesus. Did they fear imprisonment and death enough to heed the threats? No, every day after that they stood in the temple courts preaching the good news that Jesus Christ the Son of God is risen. They were pleased that they were deemed worthy of suffering for the name of Jesus whom they loved and lived for. Nothing could prevent them from speaking His name.

Peter chained and imprisoned, was it to be his end? No! God had other plans. As the chains fell from his wrists, the prison doors swung open and the guards continued to sleep, Peter must have continued to praise God, in the knowledge that his time had not yet come. Peter had more of God's work before him.

In Stephen's final moments did he call out and question why God allowed such pain? Stephen did call out, but it was not in fear or agony. Stephen called out for God to forgive the men who were throwing the stones. Stephen did not face emptiness as he closed his eyes for the last time, for just before being dragged off to be stoned he had glimpsed the wonders that awaited him. Stephen had seen God in all His glory and Jesus, whom he knew so well, sitting at the right hand of His Father. Even amidst the brutality of being stoned to death, it seems there was peace, for when he closed his eyes for the final time, he "went to sleep" and went to be in the heavenly place he had seen.

Whatever problems you face, making time to spend alone with God is never time wasted. Take your pain, fear, worries, or difficulties to Him. It is essential. It is what we need to maintain a real perspective on what we face. It is essential for maintaining our focus on our long-term future rather than our temporal hardships. It is essential to realising that we are saved, and are in the caring hands of our Father at all times.

> "Look at the birds of the air; they do not sow or reap or store away in barns, and yet your heavenly Father feeds them. Are you not much more valuable than they? Who of you by worrying can add a single hour to his life?"
>
> (Matthew 6:25-27)

> 'But seek first his kingdom, and his righteousness and all these things will be given onto you as well. Therefore do not worry about tomorrow, for tomorrow will worry about itself. Each day has enough trouble of its own."
>
> (Matthew 6:33&34)

We read in the gospels that, as Jesus faced what was to be the biggest challenge of His life, even *He* was almost overwhelmed by it. His response was to get away from it all, even from the disciples whom He left praying. There He confronted His fear. He faced the problem head on and with His Father's help He dealt with it. While He lay face down on the ground - drops of sweat and tears falling like drops of blood - He drew close to His Father. As the angel from heaven came and stood beside Him He drew strength from the certainty that His Father was there with Him. He did not come back from His time alone consumed with fear and worry. He came back to His disciples, woke them up and walked confidently to meet the kiss of His betrayer. What strength Jesus must have gained through meeting with His Father in that quiet place, to be able to walk back in the direction He knew would lead to such unimaginably deep physical, emotional and spiritual pain. But that is exactly what happened. He walked back and faced it because time had been spent in the place where it counted most. He had spent time alone with His father. And after these most difficult of times came the glorious resurrection. The greatest surprise victory the world has ever known. Jesus Christ, flogged, beaten, mocked, stabbed, nailed, tortured, and then killed, rose from the grave against all odds - against all expectations. At what point did the victory shout fill the heavens? As the grave clothes started to move? As Jesus stood up in the tomb? As the stone rolled away and Jesus looked out over a world that was changed forever? Jesus remained close to His Father during the hard times and the victory was His. It was a victory for each of us.

The problems and trials and hardships described above are in the extreme. Some of us may face such extreme hardship; some of us may not. But we all face troubled times to one degree or another. The sickness of a friend, the death of a loved one, financial problems, broken relationships, discrimination because of our faith, things going wrong, pain, depression, lack of direction in our life, redundancy, illness, the list goes on and on. It is the result of living in a fallen world. Whatever it is we face we need to bring it before God and trust in Him. God is in control of the entire universe and He is intensely interested in every detail of our lives. There is no better place to turn when times are hard.

Self-Sufficient Dependency
(Freedom From Misplaced Dependence)

"He fears no human face; no title or rank have
consideration from him alongside the interests of
his flock. No mother's passion for her child, no love
of patriot for his fatherland, could ever eclipse the
strenuous devotion [to his flock]... or the blazing
tempestuous courage of the shepherd."

(Lauchlan McLean Watt, 'The Hills of Home')

"I am the good shepherd; I know my sheep and my
sheep know me - just as the Father knows me and
I know the Father - and I lay down my life for the
sheep."

(Jesus Christ, John 10:14).

Our Saviour is the Good Shepherd, who will pursue
us no matter where we go. He showed absolute
selflessness as He walked through the darkness to
meet the kiss of Judas. He stood facing all those of rank, title
and power as they judged him a blasphemer. He stood and

listened as those He loved shouted for His blood. He showed us His love by dying so that we may live. Our Saviour, our Shepherd who has given His all for us, who stands waiting for us to turn to Him. It is our choice. We have the free will to choose, we can run to Him or we can run elsewhere. Jesus is there, continually waiting.

I clearly remember sitting on a hard pew, and staring at one of the stained glass windows at the front of the Northern Irish church I attended as a boy. There were three large windows, one depicting the return of the prodigal son, and another representing the parable of the lost coin. But it was the third that held my attention. Its fragments of coloured glass, separated by thin strips of lead, depicted a shepherd finding a lost sheep. The Shepherd stood on a little hill, reaching his staff down to the bottom of a steep drop to where a lamb gazed up and awaited rescue. The first two windows I would happily have replaced with clear glass for at the time I thought church would be less boring if I could at least see out! But the image in that third window I would have wanted to remain. It may partly have been the fact that there were some green areas that must be fields or hills, and something that looked a bit like a waterfall, and over these places of imagined freedom I could see myself running and climbing and jumping without any sight of a wooden pew! But that image of a shepherd rescuing a sheep that had been lost is an image that has stayed with me over the years. The idea that the God who created the entire universe, would actually take action to save me and that He would give me the free will to choose seems absurd. It was my choice to wander, my choice to stray and get lost, yet when I looked, there He was, standing waiting to rescue me and lead me back to the place I should be.

She runs past my friends Ross and Kirk as they tend the fire, its yellow flame flickering and the smoke keeping midges at bay. She runs past Calum as he stands looking down the valley. She passes Dan and her Grandfather as they chat and brew the tea over the little aluminium stove. Adara runs toward me, looking so small and vulnerable among these great granite boulders. She looks so small against the backdrop of mighty mountains with their heads in the clouds. She looks so small yet at the same time confident as she runs toward me on the unsteady little legs of a two-year-old.

Often she runs to me with a smile on her face like this. Other times she runs to me because she has tripped, or hurt herself, or because she is frightened. I watch her picking her way between the boulders finding her way to me. I always feel this pleasure when she chooses me, when she sees me as the one who can help her, comfort her, offer relief from her pain if only through distraction, or when she sees me as the one who can make her feel safe again. If she were lost, I would leave everything and search continually until I found her, and while I searched I would think about that moment when she sees me and a relieved smile spreads across her face. I find pleasure when my daughter needs me, calls on me, turns to me, and I can do something to help.

We cannot assume that we can please Jesus with our presence in some egotistical way, as though we have anything to offer Him. But when we turn to Him and acknowledge that only He can satisfy our needs then surely our Saviour, who died for us, would be pleased that we finally acknowledge and return His love. But it has to be our choice. When we need constant motivating just to spend time in the presence of the one we claim to love how must it feel for them? How would it feel for you if your husband or wife or children or friends needed prompting and motivating from someone else just to spend time with you? There you are standing waiting, wanting nothing more than their company, wanting to laugh with them, cry with them, and be with them, yet they walk right past you to seek the advice or help of others. I wonder how it feels for Jesus when He stands waiting and we fail to even notice Him until someone else prompts us? Or is it the hard time we hit that is the prompt: the reminder that we need someone more powerful? Even then if we run to our Saviour, at least we are acknowledging that it is only He who can help us. But even in those hard times how often do we flee firstly to those we look up to - to our leaders and our pastors - running right past the open arms of our Saviour to seek some advice or help? All the while He is there: our Saviour, the Good Shepherd, fearless, courageous, devoted to us and longing to give us all we need.

There is a serious danger for any Christian who becomes too dependent on anyone or anything else to maintain their relationship with Jesus, for what happens when that thing we depend on is removed? Conservationists and dedicated wildlife enthusiasts go to great lengths to protect endangered species from extinction. Animals are bred in captivity and released into areas from which the natural populations have been wiped out. These reintroduced animals are often fitted with radio tracking devices so that their success can be monitored. All too often the beep of the tracker indicates a stationary animal and that stationary animal usually turns out to be a corpse. Like a sea otter lying at the tide line, its only movement caused by the water that gently nudges its lifeless body to and fro. Or an eagle lying motionless except for the feathers that are ruffled by the breeze, the spark of life long gone from its jet black eyes.

The problem is that these animals have become too used to the easy food provided in captivity, and to the safety from predators provided by the fences. Their wildness has been tamed. They accept their surroundings and settle for a life of being caged in. They forget how to hunt, and how to avoid, or defend themselves against predators. They forget how to find or make their own shelter and even forget how to interact with other members of their own species. They become an easy target - food for their enemy - prey to the first foe that comes their way.

The parallel is all too apparent at times for the Christian, who seems to require regular prompting to kneel in prayer, to worship, to praise, or to read and study the word of God. When is your main time of worship in the week? Is it the Sunday morning meeting? Is that your only time of praise? What about prayer, is it five minutes at best as you drift off to sleep, or during the communal prayer meeting? What about reading and studying the scriptures? Is it your daily bread or do you try to swallow enough on a Sunday morning to get you through the week? Without the motivating, and prompting what will happen? Will we be found, spiritually dead, unmoving like the released animals? Or can we learn that our loving Saviour is there, longing to provide for all we need, longing to give us the shelter and security we seek, the nourishment that we so desperately require on a daily basis?

Not all reintroduction schemes fail. Those that are successful train the animals to do all the things they need to do in the wild. When the animals leave their cages they are ready to face the challenges ahead. They are trained to be self-sufficient, and dependent upon the wild land rather than on any human provision and protection. These animals are the successful ones and their populations rise and fill the land that was empty. While the church is certainly no cage, it is viewed by many as a place where we are fed and protected. It should be a place where we are trained to be most effective when we are outwith its boundaries, away from the body of people that comprise it. We should reach a place where we are self-sufficient in our dependency upon our Saviour, a place where we are dependent upon Him alone.

I never used to be particularly enamoured when reading the scriptures, and I would find myself being likened to a sheep. Better than being a goat I suppose, but still, why couldn't it be a stag, or an eagle or a wolf? I struggled to get excited about being likened to the docile domestic sheep, wandering around flat fenced-in fields with their dark vacant eyes and a bloated belly from too much easy food and too little activity. A line of sheep, each one with its head to the backside of the one in front, and all trudging along the same well-worn groove in the grass, failed to inspire me. And yet Jesus calls Himself the Shepherd, and us His flock.

It was in the hills that I saw the flock that is a more fitting image for followers of Jesus. Take our eyes off the flat fenced lands and look to these sheep of the hills and wild moorlands, and you will find animals that are self-sufficient in their journeys over the wildest terrain. They still remain led by and dependent upon their shepherd and are also part of a flock. But rather than walking in an ordered line of least resistance, these sheep will respond to the shepherd's call by taking the direct and difficult, often dangerous routes over any obstacle. They know the rewards are great, they know they will be led to shelter, or to where the freshest food grows. They all go in the same direction toward the shepherd, but they all tread their own path with much less of the fear and timidity associated with their domesticated counterparts. John Muir was inspired by the movement of sheep over the wildest terrain in the Sierra Nevada Mountains. He writes:

> "We may observe that the domestic sheep, in a general way, is expressionless, like a dull bundle of something only half alive, while the wild is as elegant and graceful as a deer, every movement manifesting admirable strength and character. The tame is timid; the wild is bold. The tame is almost always ruffled and dirty; while the wild is as smooth and clean as the flowers of mountain pastures."
>
> (John Muir, 'My First Summer in the Sierra')

Surely it is with boldness we are to live. Surely we are to face any obstacle head on in order to get to the great riches our Shepherd brings. Surely we are to be more like the wild sheep, for in doing so we will tread our own unique path with our sights firmly fixed on the Shepherd.

If we blindly follow those in front of us we could soon get lost or be led off the track that has been set before us. Ultimately a day will come when we will stand and give account for the decisions we have made and for the life we have led. On that day we will not be able to point the finger and blame anyone else for our shortcomings. As Paul writes: "Therefore... continue to work out your salvation with fear and trembling, for it is God who works in you to will and act according to his good purpose." (Philippians 2:12&13) Yes, we have teachers and leaders and people who hold us accountable, but the onus is on each and every one of us to work out our *own* salvation. On the hill amongst the flock, there are always certain sheep that lead and influence the general direction in which they move, knowing where the shepherd expects them to be. But the rest of the flock do not walk along in an orderly line of dull stereotypes. They each have their own path, and yet still as a whole go in the same direction. By being fully dependent upon the Shepherd, we free the leaders up to do what they need to – to look ahead and seek the right direction and to direct and lead others that way. We need to learn to follow and respect our leaders while continually being aware that God is our ultimate leader. If everybody walks along, simply following the one in front, then a well-worn groove will quickly develop. The groove is religiosity, rules and rituals followed through tradition, habit and empty action. When each individual keeps their eyes fixed upon Jesus the result is freedom and diversity within the church. It becomes a place of dynamic creativity, excitement, and effectiveness. The church becomes made up of people who are bold and strong, confidently walking toward their Saviour and following the unique path set before them. Each individual who follows Christ has been told by Him to go forth and make disciples. We need to move ourselves from a place where we are heavily dependent on those around us, to a place where we are self-sufficient in following the Shepherd. We need to mature in our faith, and in our spiritual walk. We need to change from a spiritual baby to an adult, to grow up in our faith. "Like new-born babies, crave spiritual milk, so that by it you may grow up in your salvation." (1 Peter 2:2) This is the type of church that will go forth and impact nations.

Think again about the flatland cousins of those wild woolly animals. Think about the fences that restrict them. Square patches of flat land separated from wild places by a surrounding barbed-wire fence. It holds the sheep all in one place, cosy and safe. A place where they are fed without much effort on their part. When we give our lives over to Jesus it is not like that. We do not suddenly step into a life that is cosy and safe. It was after Saul encountered God on the lonely road to Damascus that he stepped into the real adventure. Prior to his encounter Saul was on his way to Damascus to find and take as prisoners, anyone who "belonged to the way." He was already responsible for the death of many Christians. Saul had the backing of the authorities - the backing of the majority - and he had men under his command. In many ways he was safe, popular, and comfortable. But there on the dusty road a light from heaven flashed around him. Those who travelled with him stood speechless as Saul lay on the ground and the voice of Jesus told him what he must do. After this Divine meeting Saul was left blind for three days and his life took on a whole new direction. He went on to learn from those he had previously so viciously persecuted. He learned what it really meant to "belong to the way." Saul changed his name to Paul, and his life was changed even more radically. He became the persecuted one; he was beaten, thrown in prison, caught up in riots, placed under house arrest, and shipwrecked. Paul did not step into a life that was cosy and safe, but he did keep his sights fixed firmly upon Jesus who showed him the way. In doing so Paul was able to write that "to live is Christ, to die is gain." While enduring the hardships that would have many people giving up, Paul kept his sights on Jesus and as a result he endured the race with its many obstacles.

The church - that body of people we join with - should not be some safe Christian ghetto, separated from the world around. We should be set apart, yes, but not closed off. I know that when I turned to the open arms of my Saviour, my life expanded. Now it is fuller than I ever imagined it could be. There are more surprises along the way, and I revel in a heightened sense of adventure. The real adventure, the real wildness, comes as soon as we step into the ultimate freedom that has been bought for us. Things are rarely calm and cosy. We still have to overcome obstacles and face hard times. Those things are still there and may even increase. The difference is that we have our sights firmly set on the great Shepherd who is leading the way to a place where there will be no troubles. We move with purpose, and every step taken is a step closer to Him. Our path is no longer a random wander interspersed with regular hardships that get us down. Instead we move constantly toward our goal. The Shepherd awaits, showing the way.

Brown coat glistens as the sleek muscular form of the otter dives and swims. Such graceful movement at the Atlantic's edge. Elegance as he swims through moon-pulled tides. A picture of health and agility, living his life where land meets ocean.

And over snow-covered summits the eagle flies. Rising over ridges, gliding through valleys. Those keen dark eyes shining with life. Golden feathers glow in the evening's setting sun. A shadow cast against pure-white snow, moving fast and free, as over wild landscapes the great bird soars.

Beyond the Trees

"Anyone who listens to the word but does not do
what it says is like a man who looks at his face in a
mirror and, after looking at himself, goes away and
immediately forgets what he looks like".

(James 1:23&24)

If we go to someone and tell them we are thirsty, and
they respond by describing a spring where wonderfully
clear, pure, water pours from beneath the earth, their
words would do nothing to quench our thirst. In fact they
may even make us thirst more. We may long with all our
heart to drink deeply from the pool described, but we would
be no more hydrated as a result of the description. And if we
were cold - shiveringly cold - with numb fingers and toes?
A picture of a roaring fire would do nothing to warm us.
Our digits would stay numb despite the image of the fire
filling our minds. And if we were hungry? The description
of a delicatessen with all its finest meats, wines, cheeses,
breads, and sweet pastries may cause the mouth to water,

but the words would not fill an empty stomach.

Remember the fictional nation mentioned at the beginning of these freedom chapters - the one so densely covered in trees? It is the place where the majority of the inhabitants spend their lives between the trunks, under the shading branches and canopy of leaves. The place where only some of the inhabitants long to know what lies hidden beyond the leafy roof. Their longing to know is so strong that they start to climb, to do what they would not normally do, to do that which is perceived as dangerous. They climb up through the branches until they can push their faces through the canopy. And as they do, they realise that the pure brilliance above surpasses all their expectations, all they had hoped and longed for. And they also know that their description of it will fall far short of its actual brilliance. They may convey a little of it through their excited words and their shining faces, but to really grasp it, to know it, to feel it, they know that the experience has to be firsthand. They know that to really get it, their companions must climb up through the branches themselves until they too can peer into the realm that causes their faces to shine as they reflect the brilliant light above.

Freedom has been our focus over the past few chapters. Now we need to experience it firsthand; we need to think about it, dream about it, and live it! We need to start revelling in the freedom that God has bought for us. It is time to reach up, grab the branches and start moving towards the brilliant light.

THE CALL

Learning To Walk

"The Lord is my shepherd, I shall not be in want. He
makes me lie down in green pastures, he leads me
beside quiet waters, he restores my soul."
(Psalm 23:1-3)

R est and be Thankful. This is the name given to a place
on the West Coast of Scotland. On my first visit there,
I was with Lindsay, and what we found was quite
unexpected...

We had initially set out that day to reach the rocky
pinnacle that forms the summit of a hill known as 'The
Cobbler' (Ben Arthur) on Scotland's West coast. Even at the
loch-side car park the wind howled and growled through the
valley. The Spruce forest that stretched up the slopes hid the
path that would take us from the loch-side and onto the open
mountainside above. The trees swayed in unison flashing
the lighter underside of their dark needles in response to the
conducting wind.

Across the road and up through the swaying sea of green
we climbed. Everywhere there was noise and movement: the
evidence of an unseen force that made even the damp, dark,
misty world under the evergreen seem like a refuge. Soon
however, the refuge dropped below and became a distant part
of an expanding view as we trod a well-worn path upwards.
It led us to the huge 'Narnain boulders'. These house-sized

pieces of rock provided us with a brief shelter and are a place to which I have since returned on many occasions.

As we rested at these boulders we started to feel the wind-driven cold. We walked on, hoping that movement would warm us. On into the mist through which we were allowed only brief tantalising glimpses of the rocky pillars above. It was the usual incredible feeling up on the hillside, with this awesome force whipping the mist around us and these huge boulders and rock faces with aeons of time locked within. Despite the exhilarating feelings the wind and cold soon teamed up and the growl and howl and nip became a bite. It was time to retreat.

Back at sea level and in the car we noticed on the map that the road led up a valley to the 'Rest and be Thankful'. I had heard of it or read of it before and so off we headed thinking of a cosy hotel or café where soup and coffee would provide some inner heat and a roaring fire would warm us. What we found was a rugged windswept car park overlooking the loch below and hills beyond. No soup or warming drink like we had been hoping for! I later discovered that Lindsay and I were not the first people to arrive at the 'Rest and be Thankful' with the wrong expectations. The poet Keats and his friend Charles Brown had been heading that way in 1818 and on that occasion had apparently walked fifteen miles hoping to enjoy breakfast at what they thought was an Inn called The Rest and be Thankful! At least Lindsay and I had a car. We simply changed our plans for the second time that day, as dictated by the weather and the landscape, and went elsewhere. The weather had been harsh, we did not reach the pointy summit we had set out for, and we did not find what we were looking for at the Rest and be Thankful. We did however, return home with memories of a great day spent together in Scotland's wild landscape. Natural places are largely outwith man's control. It is a large part of their appeal provided we can learn to allow our plans and expectations to be altered without disappointment, and learn to take pleasure in adapting to wilderness instead of trying to adapt it to suit us.

Another of my visits to the 'Narnain Boulders' was with

my friend Simon and our objective was a more precarious route to the eastern summit known among rock climbers as 'The Recess Route'. Our fairly new harnesses, ropes, guidebook and climbing gadgets proved invaluable. As did our minimal knowledge gained through a few shorter rock climbs and a book called 'Learn to Climb in a Weekend'! While we had gained some knowledge and experience, it was nowhere near enough. This is not an approach to encountering God in the wilderness that I would recommend!

It was my most recent visit to that rugged West Coast corner that had the most profound impact upon me spiritually. Through the trees and up the well-worn, and now well-known, path I walked. This time the trees were still, as was the air. On my back I carried enough food and equipment for two days in this environment. Despite having more time I had no summit as my aim, and certainly was not going to try any more of the areas' rock climbs. I had no pre-set agenda other than to rest and spend time with God. I wandered, soaking in the smells of the heather-clad slopes, hearing the larks above me and the stream beside. The jagged rock peaks contrasting with the greens and browns of the heather, framed by the blue of the sky, caused me to pause regularly and drink through every sense. My wandering brought me back to the Narnain Boulders and once again they surprised me with their size. Many critics claim that mountain or wilderness writers tend to exaggerate or romanticise their experience like the fisherman's 'one that got away'. I find that my own memory of such sites and places does quite the opposite. It is as though my mind is limited in the amount of detail and scale and wonder it can capture.

Lunch beside the boulders - then where? A quick browse of the map, and I decided to head on along the valley. Another breathtaking pause, more due to the impact of the view than the effects of effort. Up to my right I noticed a huge boulder-filled hollow in the side of the hill. The route I had decided just a few minutes ago was quickly forgotten and off toward the rock-strewn hollow I headed with the familiar excited sense of exploration of a new area. Up, through, over and even under these huge rocks I went, jumping, climbing, squeezing, zig zagging here and there, intrigue leading ever upward physically and spiritually. I was now headed east rather than west but it mattered not. I was delighted by thoughts that I was possibly the first person in years to look amongst the rocks into hidden nooks and crannies.

These nooks and crannies contained some little plants; growing in millimetres of soil and receiving just a few hours of light a day. I kept sauntering about, then sitting and looking and as I did, I felt the presence of God as clearly as I ever have. I was appreciating more of the small individual parts of an immense whole. I was learning more about God through what He has made. I did not feel worthy of such intimacy with such immensity. Here I was, being shown aspects of the Creator through His creation. My only response was pleasure at the heart knowledge I was gaining, followed by praise because of it. Knowledge of what Jesus has done for me. His sacrifice upon the cross was like those millimetres of soil and few rays of light, for they allowed life to exist where really none should.

It seems almost frightening to think back on this time and how easily I could have rushed past and missed such revelation. John Muir appears to have recognised the danger in overlooking what God has provided. He comments that 'hiking is a vile word' and that the only way to approach wilderness is 'to saunter'. Leave agendas and goals behind. Instead saunter, and let yourself be led by a sense of exploration through creation. Set out to meet with God. That should be your expectation and it should grow with every step you take away from the towns and cities. Go out to walk the dog, and the dog will be walked. Sit and look at a pleasant view and that is what you will do. Go out with the sole intention of gaining a summit or a certain number of miles and you will probably succeed in your quest. To do these things without really looking and considering what is around, and without the desire to meet God there, means that you will miss out on the real joy that is to be gained through creation. Go with the intention of meeting God, allowing Him to change and free you, seek new levels in the spiritual realm, and that will be your experience. Purpose affects, even dictates, experience.

Through rushing we miss so much and appreciate even less. When we rush through the natural creation in a superficial way, we miss most of what it has to offer. It is like rushing past a news stand; maybe we grab a headline as we pass, but we fail to really understand the article because we do not take the time to read the small print.

The headline is clearly seen, bold and eye-catching, even breathtaking. Those rolling hills all shades of green and brown and mist-shrouded grey. Purple at the right time of year, pure-white a little later. It is that column of white water that cascades from rocky heights to crash against the valley floor. It's those dark storm clouds moving intimidatingly across the sky, dwarfing mighty mountains. It's the flashes of lighting as they unleash their fury, the rumble and thump of thunder that shakes the hills. It's that sea of green that stretches out across the lower slopes. Those trees swaying in unison as the sunlight floods across their leaves. It is the vast sea stretching out to a curving horizon - that point where sea and sky appear to join. It is that golden path across the rippling surface. It's those powerful waves that slam against the coastline, hurling themselves onto beaches, shifting tons of sand with a single sweep, blasting rock that is being constantly worn by their relentless action. It is the world turned white as the winter snows fall. It is the glowing green of sunlit summer, the flowering colour of spring and the rusty browns, reds and golds of autumn. It is that banner of star-strewn vastness that dwarfs, humbles, inspires and leaves us awe-struck on a cloudless night.

But under the headlines is the article containing the detail. That which through looking closer, through studying, brings a fuller understanding of the whole. The detail, like the single leaf falling as another season passes and with it time. I read what it says about the transience of life, yet at the same time the promise that new life awaits. The detail is in the patterns in the rock grain, pressed together by incomprehensible forces. Colossal forces over which mankind has no control - yet there is such order. The small-print is in the diversity of colour on a single lichen-covered rock. So diverse yet all blended to look so natural and in keeping with what has been made. It says that it is the work of a Creator who knows the whole picture, who sees how all of life on earth fits together. It is the fine spray spreading out from below a waterfall, and the droplets of water that form on the leaves of the plants they touch. From there they drip to water the earth and nourish the roots. I read it, and understand a little of what it says about our God of abundant provision. It is the heavy raindrops bouncing off leaves so forcefully that all the dust is washed away. And after the rain, it is the first faint rays of sunlight that illuminate a glistening world. I read it, I read about the washing away of sin in our lives; the second chance we have been given through love so powerful and grace beyond measure. It is the water that drips from my hand, back into the sea from where it was taken. A literal drop in the ocean, like my years on earth set within the vast sea of eternity and grasped a fraction more through reading the small-print of a single drop. It is each individually shaped snowflake, so delicate, yet joining to dramatically transform the whole landscape. It is the tiny buds on the tip of each branch, and all the energy of spring. It is the new shoots pushing up from the dark earth, the frost patterns on a winter's morning, the breath swirling through cold air. So much I read but do not yet fully understand. So much felt rather than known. So much of God in His wonderful creation. So much beauty that is the merest hint of what is to come.

When we understand the value of getting into creation, there are many practical steps we can take so that our times there are as safe and comfortable as possible, meaning that we can relax and apply ourselves to the spiritual exercise more fully. The following are some basic practicalities that may help you get the most out of your time alone amidst creation. There are also some points to keep in mind if you intend going on a more ambitious walk:

Follow a path and then follow it back again.If there is no path, then follow a burn or river and then follow it back. Walk round a loch. Think practically when planning a route. Leave a note of your planned location with your wife or husband,or with a family member or friend. Begin with short easy strolls and as you gain confidence you can start to aim for higher and more remote areas. Spend time with others learning the ropes or reading 'how to' books before venturing out into the wildest areas alone. Learn to read a map. Use common sense. Get familiar with an area, because familiarity enables us to relax more and be less distracted by concerns. In saying that, exploration of new areas is also a great thing, for God's creation is diverse. Just take your time and get used to moving over and through wild terrain. All these small practical steps will lead to a more successful time spiritually, as you can relax and focus on this deeper purpose for being in the wild location.

Wear sensible clothing. The outdoor clothing industry is huge and every taste and requirement is catered for. Thankfully not all waterproofs come in fluorescent colours these days! But you don't have to go to the nearest outdoor shop and drain your bank accounts to head out into the wild. You do not really need any extra clothing to go for a walk in the park during your lunch break. The farther, and particularly the higher you go, then the more gear you will require. Having the right gear does allow for more comfort when the weather turns nasty. Much of the time the weather will be fine and starting small means that if it turns bad you will not have far to get back to shelter. Warm clothing, a waterproof jacket if you have it, and a sturdy pair of shoes with good grips is enough to get you out into wild creation. After all, man has been roaming the hills long before 'breathable waterproofs' and fleece jackets were invented!

Take a mobile with you but leave it switched off. Keep it as an emergency back up. Remember also that it won't work in many wild sites so do not rely upon it too heavily. The best mobile phone to take is the one that lies unused and forgotten at the bottom of our rucksack. Our main aim is to go and commune with God, not the people we have left back home. If you feel the urge to make a call, stop and consider whether it is urgent enough to break up your time of peace and stillness. Don't let it become an unnecessary distraction.

Do not be disappointed if you go out and have no flashing light, voice from the clouds type, intensely spiritual experience. Sometimes it does feel like you simply walk and pray, and come away with no grand revelation. Sometimes it is only with hindsight that you realise how deep the experience has been or even days, weeks or months afterwards you will hear a certain topic spoken about and realise you have a heart knowledge of it. Or you will be singing a hymn or song of praise and realise there is an added depth to your words. That heart knowledge and added depth can often be traced back to the time with God amidst creation, that time when you didn't feel that much was going on!

Don't use the wonders of wild creation to gloss over issues that you need to deal with. Sometimes you just want to praise God for His glory revealed through creation but as your mind continually returns to niggling thoughts and concerns, it feels as though there is a wrestling match going on in your mind. Sometimes those niggling thoughts are things we need to face up to and deal with. We keep pushing them aside and try to simply praise, while they are the very things God wants us to deal with.

As said in the earlier chapter 'A Few Words of Caution', never misplace your hope in nature itself. Without God you will find it empty. Nature is God's creation. Through it we learn of Him, it helps us draw near to Him, and it inspires our worship and stirs our praise of Him.

I could continue to promote the beauty of nature and write of the joys to be found in meeting God there using every positive word the dictionary contains, and you could go out with great expectations and still what you experience would overwhelm and dwarf those expectations. What will God reveal to you? How will time alone with Him change your life? What will you miss if you don't set aside the time? Sometimes there is a fine line between doing something and not doing something, and that fine line has consequences for the whole of life!

I remember setting off for a time alone, and wondering if I was going with too much expectation. In the dark of the early morning I left the car by the roadside and set off by bicycle along the gravel track that would eventually lead me to a high belach between two even higher hills. As I rode I wondered if I had hyped it all up too much in my mind. I left the bike at the belach and headed up over a summit on foot, dropping down into an isolated valley on the other side. Still the little nagging doubt in my mind – was I expecting too much?

A burn provided a fresh cold drink and as I sat down beside it I heard a stag call out across the valley. And there it was before me, standing in that stereotypical pose, seen in so many photographs, with head held high and antlers pointing to the heavens. Across the river a second stag called in response, a deep sound that seemed to fill the whole valley. One stag called, and the other answered. I could only see the one closest to me. The one across the valley was too far away, and it blended in too well with the landscape. As I sat there, cut off from civilisation by the surrounding mountains, I felt goose bumps rise all over my body. I was calling to God. I could not see Him directly, but I knew He was with me, answering, calling to me, calling me to Him. With each of the stag's deep calls I felt more privileged to be there, and more aware of the glory of God. I knew for certain that my concerns about expecting too much were unfounded.

Meeting God in His wild creation yet again surpassed all expectations.

The rest of the day I continued to move in that attitude of praise and prayer. High on a ridge and yet again, shrouded in cloud I felt as though the cloud represented God's presence, filling every nook and cranny in the rocks and filling my vision no matter where I looked. Occasionally the cloud would clear to reveal the many lochs of wild Rannoch Moor, a vast expanse of trackless country, beautiful in its ruggedness. On these occasions I would stop and stare, feeling like Moses when God passed before him high on the rocky slopes of Sinai. My response to seeing such glory was to praise out loud, and to be alone in that remote place and speaking out loud felt like the most natural thing in the world.

The personal experiences described in this book I hope will inspire more Christians to get out there into wild creation. I have written of times and places where all was perfect, great weather, no midges, beautiful surroundings and the sense of elation throughout. I have also included hard times: times when I have been as cold as it feels possible to get, or lost and scared - but all are times when I have drawn nearer to God and developed spiritually through the experience. The only negative wild experiences have been times when I headed out with my own agenda, trying to find freedom, happiness or direction without looking first to God. The best of times are there to be reached for and taken, and all we have to do to have a positive wild experience is to look to God, and seek Him first. These are the experiences of genuine transcendence, when we leave the plain of 'here and now' and find ourselves on a plain where everything is viewed as evidence of the greatest love of all. It is a place where we can learn our own position in the grand scheme of things, a place where we can find all the deep things we genuinely long for. There within God's beautiful landscapes we can develop a deeper heart-relationship with God our Father.

Spiritual Expeditions
Meeting God Amidst Creation

"Expedition: a journey or voyage for a particular
purpose."
(Oxford Concise English Dictionary)

"Jesus went out as usual to the Mount of Olives...
knelt down and prayed."
(Luke 22:39&41)

Anyone can go on their own expedition, to journey
out into natural settings to pray and be alone before
their heavenly Father. But to help people experience
wilder places or to further kindle their desire to be amidst
such places, it can be a good thing to be lead. 2005 saw the
birth of 'Spiritual Expeditions.' These expeditions offer an
opportunity to go a bit further into the wild landscape, to
explore more of creation, to climb a bit higher, to taste a
bit more adventure. For those less experienced in travel
over wilder ground the expeditions offer an opportunity to
experience this sense of freedom while feeling safe through
being led by people who are trained, qualified and well
experienced. 'Spiritual Expeditions' are organized times

away from the busyness and routine of everyday life. They range in duration from single days to weekends and their specific aim is for individuals to meet with God through and amidst the creation He has made.

These expeditions have developed rapidly in the short time they have been running. But even during the first expeditions, God has met powerfully and intimately with those who set aside time to be with Him in the midst of what He has made.

'There and Back Again!'
An Account of the First 'Spiritual Expedition'

People not where they should be. People where they should be but at the wrong times. People where they should be and at the right time, but with all the wrong kit - or no kit at all. An hour after we should have been heading north west, here we are heading south east to collect someone who got the information about where to meet completely wrong. At last we find him, with nothing but the clothes on his back, smiling, eager to be on his way for an overnight Spiritual Expedition. Thankfully I brought spare kit! At last we are heading north – on a different road from the one planned - and much later - but at least we are on our way!

It is a minibus full of very different people: a surgeon, a joiner, a leisure centre manager, a head teacher, students, and some unemployed are the range of occupations and backgrounds present. Their personalities differ even more! Some have been Christians for only a week or two, some haven't yet fully decided, while others have been Christians longer than I have been alive. Some are almost twice my age, some not much more than half.

There is an excited and slightly awkward conversation going on between people who do not know each other very well, but who are united by the fact they are heading together into unfamiliar territory. Some laugh and joke together, while others, I can see in the rear view mirror, appear to be looking around with an expression of puzzlement upon their brow! As the surgeon produces a mouth organ I can see those lines of puzzlement deepening. Their thoughts of 'what on earth am I doing here?' can be read clearly on their faces!

Above the mouth organ and occasional lines of song, the smokers can be heard calling for a cigarette break. (We have only travelled about ten miles as the first calls are heard). I focus on the road, trying to ignore the smokers' shouts and also the stomach cramps caused by an early dinner eaten too quickly. I also try to focus and pray about this expedition, but my thoughts and prayers are regularly interrupted by facts about parrots. Yes parrots! One of the group is a parrot expert, seemingly knowing all there is to know about parrots, and determined that by the end of our journey we will all share such knowledge. I listen quietly, and genuinely find it interesting until our parrot expert decides to tell us, word for word, his 'African Grey's' foul-mouthed (or foul-beaked) repertoire! At this point I feel the need to quickly change the subject.

The mouth organ is in operation again and its operator is also attempting to rouse some songs. Getting the group to sing is difficult. Getting them to sing in the same key and in time is entirely impossible. My idea of a group of people eager to meet God amidst His creation has almost evaporated, like the clouds of cigarette smoke at the last toilet stop. I find myself in silent prayer, fighting against thoughts that this expedition would be a disaster in terms of any spiritual significance. My mind has almost written it off as a failure... 'The group is just too mixed'... 'Some are just too new to it all'... 'They are too wild'... 'I don't know how to speak to such a mixed group'... 'I don't know how to lead them' and so forth are the thoughts in a mind, too restricted by logic and reason. Yet in my heart I still have a glimmer of hope. Driving through the darkness, with great black silhouettes of mountains all around, I switch off to the sounds around me. I close my mind to the conversations in the back and pray, desperately, that this time away will glorify God. The miles roll past as I pray for each of the group.

The final few miles follow a roller-coaster road to the

end of a valley where the road stops abruptly in a narrow car park cut into the hillside. It is almost midnight by the time we reach the end of our drive and the start of our journey on foot. Packs on, a quick chat, emphasizing that we are not here as hill walkers, climbers, campers or any other such thing, but that we are setting off into the night as followers of Jesus Christ, and that in walking out into wild creation to meet with our Father, we are emulating Jesus. Soon we settle into a reasonable pace, following torch beams through the moonless night. The rough path winds up along the side of a deep wooded gorge. The river can be heard tumbling with a roar down its steep course toward the sea. Leafless trees reach skyward. Birch, Pine, Alder, Rowan, they all look the same in the darkness. The path is, in places, is little more than a ledge cut from near-vertical slopes of the very flanks of some of Scotland's highest mountains.

Soon we emerge from the forest and out into an open valley. The group gathers together and we switch off our torches. All around us are the dark silhouettes of huge mountains set against a star-filled sky. We stand amazed. A diverse group, standing united in awe of the vast night sky stretching out above us. I shout out Psalm 19. My voice fades away into the night, and together we stand, humbled by the greatness of God's creation, listening to the language it speaks.

After a while we move on, trying to find the driest route through very marshy ground. Eventually we find the bridge, though to call it a bridge is somewhat misleading. It consists of three wires stretched across the river, all of which sway alarmingly under weight. Two wires are stretched at shoulder height, an arms span apart, and are for gripping onto with white knuckled hands. The third wire is for shuffling feet. Beyond the bridge we can see our destination: the remote mountain hut with gaslights, heating and a dry place to sit and drink hot tea and coffee.

Sleep comes quickly for most of us, then the next morning we are up and out into the rain-filled valley. I head out first and watch as people emerge into the daylight and see the valley for the first time. Most have a stunned look on their face and are left speechless as they gaze upon the grandeur. The flat grass-covered valley floor, the towering cliffs rising to meet snow-capped summits and the valley stretching out for miles into the wilderness. Nearby, a huge waterfall cascades hundreds of feet to crash against the black rocks at its base. Patches of woodland reach up the valley sides, while through them flow numerous icy rivers. Again the group stands united in breathless wonder at God's creation.

The morning is activity-based, consisting of an exploration of the giant house-sized boulders that the river has cut from the earth and carved over centuries. We clamber over them, squeeze under them, edge across logs jammed between them, suspended over the frothing water. Some of the younger members of the group are determined to explore further. I watch them jumping across slippery boulders and feel a battle inside. I enjoy seeing them so animated, so fully alive in this wild setting, but I also feel responsible for bringing them back safely. At one point I fear that they have gotten themselves stuck, and cautiously make my way across the river to help them. Just as I lean across and reach out my hand I discover that they are not stuck, but have stopped for another smoke-break!

At this stage the expedition had gone well. Stunning scenery had been marveled at. The sense of adventure was there, and the challenges of the terrain had been enjoyed. After some hot soup and bread we reached the crux of our wild time. It was the time when we would all head off alone to spend time with God. After another short chat about this being the most important part of our time away, I watch as people head off in their various directions. I walk back towards the mountain hut and prepare dinner so that it would be ready a few hours later when, hopefully, everyone would return safely.

I then wandered up through the Birch-woods praying as I went. The rain had poured down continually since our arrival in the valley, and now it was as heavy as ever. Burns that were normally little more than a trickle, now flowed fast and foamed white, each one like a white ribbon draped across the vibrant green moss carpet. I climbed up to a ledge below an overhanging cliff face. From this perch I could look out over the treetops and revel in the peace and stillness of the valley. I do not remember how long I stayed there - time is of less importance in wild places. Our schedule is governed by weather, daylight, and hunger instead of the tick of the clock. Eventually with a smile on my face and a rumble in my stomach, I wandered back toward the mountain hut.

I was still unsure as to how successful an experience this would be for people in a spiritual sense. When eventually everyone did return, we sat down around basic wooden tables to eat together. Under the warm glow and faint hiss of the gaslights I asked if anyone would like to share about their lone experience during the afternoon. Previous meal-times had been noisy affairs, when chat was regularly interrupted and conversation disjointed. Now as each person shared there was absolute stillness and silence. Everyone listened intently as each person took their turn to share. There were no interruptions. Not a word was missed. Some spoke of new revelations of God's love. Some with tears rolling down their cheeks spoke of how their life would be different from this point on. Some spoke of their faith going deeper than it ever had before and some told how they realized more fully how incredible the sacrifice Jesus has made for them is. Everyone shared of a profound encounter with the living God. I sat in the electric stillness and listened, stunned, to the testimonies of people who I thought had missed the whole point of the expedition. As I listened I regularly had to hold back tears as the depth of their experience was shared.

As people spoke, I occasionally looked around at the faces of the others. They sat captivated by every word. I looked at the faces of people from very different backgrounds who had just spent an afternoon being still among God's creation and all had a story to tell. Where they had come from did not matter. In the wild landscape much was stripped away or revealed as insignificant, leaving just the real individual and their desire to know more of God.

After everyone had shared we set off across the wire bridge for a final time. The rain had fallen continually, and continued to do so. Summit snows continued to melt and below my feet, and the swaying wire, a dramatically swollen river flowed rapidly past. We gazed at the open valley for a final time before we arrived under the dripping canopy of the forest.

Soon, wet kits are thrown in the back of the bus and wet people occupy the seats. Wet, cold, tired and very happy. Back along the roller-coaster road we go. It occurs to me that I now drive a busload of very different people than those I had brought here just a day earlier. All have spoken of that change, and it is evident to varying degrees. The whole atmosphere on the bus has changed. The mouth organ pipes up again and some voices join in their varying keys. I feel more alive than ever, and smile my way through the journey home.

In Other Words

"I feel all thin, sort of *stretched*, if you know what
I mean: like butter that has been scraped over too
much bread. That can't be right. I need a change, or
something... I want to see mountains again, Gandalf
– *mountains.*"

(The Lord of the Rings, J. R. R. Tolkien)

Tolkien's hobbits are creatures that love their home
comforts and safe routines. Anything that disturbs
their peace or upsets their way of life is viewed
negatively and avoided where possible. But not for the hobbit
Bilbo Baggins. Bilbo had tasted wild adventure. He had been
places, seen sights and met people that his kinsfolk could
not even imagine. As a result Bilbo could never again fully
settle into a life of mundane comforts and daily routines. He
felt torn, stretched between the home he had always known
and a longing to be off on another adventure.

It is similar for many of us. Once we taste real intimacy
with God we long for more. We long to gaze upon the various
sights of His creation. I have seen people stand in awe of
what God has made. I have seen people get to know God
more through His creation. I have heard their praise and

worship ring out through valleys and rise up from among the trees. I have seen people on their knees among autumn leaves. I have heard their prayers spoken out, echoing across the treetops. I have had the pleasure of listening to many testimonies of life-changing, life-enhancing encounters with God amidst His creation. These encounters compel us to shirk off our comforts, and cause us to turn our backs on worldly distractions. Like Jesus we walk into wild places for the sole purpose of spending time with our loving Father. We cannot settle for any less, for if we do, we soon start to feel weak, thin, 'like butter that has been scraped across too much bread!'

Whole books could be filled with testimonies from people who have experienced God in this way. The section that follows however contains just a few testimonies from friends and family. They have all tasted a bit more adventure, seen a bigger picture, and been freed from distractions and busyness to find the peace that comes through meeting intimately with God.

I was not always a believer in the importance of the outdoors! I think I saw the idea of meeting with God in the midst of nice scenery as an option among many. Essentially, such experiences were for people of a certain persuasion and inclination – wild, mountain climbing, bothy-dwelling types! I am a convert for a number of reasons.

Firstly, one of the most amazing spiritual breakthroughs of my life came from a number of hours spent in the hills. Having normally associated such times on my own as a little lonely and melancholy, I was taken aback by the powerful nature of the experience. On a cold and bleak early spring day with not a soul in sight I was able to pray continually and powerfully for a number of hours in surroundings that seemed to add to the depth of my praying. Emerging from a difficult period of depression, fear and anxiety I felt the presence of God coming to strengthen and encourage and envision me in a way that was simply not possible in the environment of a living room. Shouting aloud to God unrestrained by 'what will the neighbors think?', declaring the truth of scripture with conviction on the top of a hill, sensing the bigger picture whilst taking in a beautiful panoramic view – all these things served to begin a transforming work that has been ongoing for a few years.

Secondly, I've come to the conclusion that where possible, praying outdoors is far more effective and definitely more pleasant. I've found that starting the day with a prayer walk is almost an essential part of the morning – as essential as putting on your clothes to go to work! These times, walking in a local public park or along the nearby cycle path have become precious to me and definitely beats falling asleep in front of the fire at home! Similarly, getting away on a Saturday morning for an extended time of prayer, contemplation and seeking God is far more refreshing than a lie-in at the weekend.

Thirdly, it's the conviction that there are certain elements in the outdoors that actually foster spiritual awakening. Things like time – it seems to stand still more when you're outdoors. I've found that giving God an extended period of time to speak is far more honoring than a 'slot' in the day.

The physical space, as well, can bring a sense of magnitude and scale when out in the open and lends itself to thinking about the enormity of God and His purposes. And while praying for other people's needs and situations it is easy to gain a more profound perspective.

I find the solitude beneficial. Losing the fear of being on my own with God has been so crucial to my relationship with Him. Of course you can experience God in your living room but there are so many distracting and falsely 'comforting' things around. I've really been blessed by confronting my apparent 'aloneness'.

The wildness itself stirs and inspires me. There's something about rugged terrain that makes me want to be as wild as my Father is! It speaks to me about adventure. It really encourages me to get back into the challenges of daily life with a renewed sense of vigor, excitement and determination to make a real difference this side of eternity.

('The Great Outdoors', Lenny Turk)

I don't think that it's possible for me to be in the hills and not be humbled by it all.

There is something about the vastness of the great outdoors that brings it out in me. Here, the clutter that life can sometimes become does not distract me. I feel a freedom to be still and appreciate the splendour of God's creation: from epic cinematic views of mountain ranges to the single blade of grass I find myself focusing on. God created both. From the rugged and the powerful to the delicate and the beautiful. He did it all.

I can feel lost and yet at home at the same time. I am alone but in the presence of something amazing – someone amazing. God is alive; here I feel alive. God is not a distant God. God is here now as He was before I. He'll be here when I am long gone too."

(David Hamilton)

I cannot remember when the snow fell. It was not that moment of waking up and opening the curtains to find a perfectly fitting blanket of white had transformed the landscape. Nor was it the picturesque, romantic walk in the snow among the evergreen trees of Airthrey Estate and looking down from the hillside which assured me of God's plan for my life. Something deeper and longer lasting established itself in my mind and soul that Advent time.

Not only did the snow fall in December that year, but it lay and remained on the fields, hills and trees for weeks. The loch froze and the passing days yielded the certainty that its surface would sustain the weight of skaters. Their silhouette-like figures etched out patterns on the ice like a nib upon a wax tablet.

But it was another work of art that was crafted in those weeks which caught my attention. The trees became transformed. Their leaves long gone, their thin, naked branches would in other years have been briefly clothed in a white cotton fall of snow. Instead, they had become white sculptures, standing gracefully and majestically around the solid water. One day, as I walked into this arena, I was awe-struck. The Artist had planned this display and had arranged a viewing for this city girl. He reached inside me to bring out an emerging appreciation for his handiwork. I began to see his hand working delicately in my life with the same attention to detail, originality and certainty of purpose.

('Trees Transformed', Louise Parmar)

Out in the wild, I met with God in a way I have never experienced before.

Much of my understanding of God's power comes from the Bible. I have come across words such as 'powerful' and 'thunderous', but I have always just read them simply as words and never completely felt their true meaning.

While away for a weekend with some friends, I was climbing a mountain in the dark, with only my rucksack and a torch. It was exciting, but to be honest I was just looking forward to getting back to the comfort of my own home. We stopped halfway up, turned off our torches and looked up at the sky. All I could see was the silhouette of the mountains lit only by the moon and stars.

I began to reflect on everything that I have in my hometown. I have my job, my comfortable home, video shops, coffee shops etc; no wonder I didn't understand the full extent of God's power. It is all too often clouded by the man-made surroundings and comforts we so easily enjoy.

As I began to walk to the bothy that evening, even though it was dark I was aware that God's creation was surrounding me, and I felt vulnerable and humbled by it all.

The first glimpse of the valley in daylight is a moment I will never forget. All around were immense mountains, pounding waterfalls, flowing rivers and many trees. The force of the water pouring powerfully towards the river again showed me God's power. I was struck with the realization that this is God's creation, and even walking across the river would have probably knocked me off of my feet.

When I found a quiet peaceful place alone, I was hit with a powerful revelation. I discovered a ledge that was big enough for me to snuggle into, and below it was a river, with the majestic mountains surrounding me. I didn't need to do anything other than simply remain there, and I felt God's stillness immediately. As I lay there, I began to think about the busyness of my life, in which I all too often fail to make time to really feel God's still, peaceful nature. I remained there for approximately an hour, but afterwards it felt like I had been on a holiday for a fortnight, as I felt completely refreshed.

I now look back in awe of that time with God and with a realization that one of the most powerful and genuine ways to experience God is

to get out into the wilderness and be confronted with His creation."
(Alan Bell)

I have never really been one for seeking solitude or looking to nature in order to gain more wisdom from God. I know some people when faced with a problem just take themselves off to meet with God in some wild place. I had never thought that way.

I suppose that is why I felt slightly confused when I did feel the urge to get outside to pray, and to seek direction for the problem I was facing. Nothing else seemed to give me any clarity. All day the urge of going out for a walk kind of niggled at me. Eventually I gave in, and found that it was the best thing I could have done.

The area around where I lived seemed very built up and uninspiring. But through wandering, I came across a little river amidst all the man-made structures. I stopped and listened to the sound of the river and watched it as it flowed gently past. I climbed down the riverbank. I wanted to sit still beside the river and the little waterfall. Almost immediately I felt the tightness that had been in my chest ease. It was as though all the stress and agitation flowed away with the water!

When I started to pray I felt closeness to God and in that place there was no room for fear. It was as though all my senses had awakened to what God had placed around me and within me. The river was peaceful with its melodic tune. I could hear the wind and feel it moving around me and see it moving the tree branches. Everything seemed new and unique, as though I had never seen it before.

I realized how little I notice of God's creation, until I surround myself with it. So often I remain blind to it because most of my time is spent in towns and cities. Lying in my room, I try to pray and seek God, but there are too many distractions. The television seems to call out to be switched on. The computer is right next to me just wanting to be used. The stereo is there ready to fill the room with music.

When I removed myself from all of this, I felt the peace that I longed for as I drew closer to God. Being outside brought clarity. The fresh air awakened me and my mind was cleared. I breathed more easily and found myself less distracted and more able to listen. God taught me a lot through that single time meeting with Him beside the river.

(Hazel McShane)

I can quite clearly remember my first strong desire to climb to the top of a mountain, or more accurately in this case, a large hill. I was walking along the side of the hill in the company of my father. We were there to further my father's pastime of training gun dogs. I cannot be sure what age I was, but I do remember edging up the hill to get nearer the top, while my father remained resolutely at the bottom where the rabbits were more plentiful. I hoped he wouldn't notice that I was becoming an even smaller dot on the hill but he must have remained alert and concerned for I know it was not until many years later that I finally reached the top of that particular hill.

I can place more accurately another and even more important event in my life. At the age of ten I came under the influence of a Godly and very evangelical Sunday school teacher, who by use of some good Ulster hellfire and damnation preaching brought me to a point where I committed my life to Christ.

Like most, if not all Christians, my spiritual life has been a series of highs and lows, but thankfully God in His patience and mercy, held onto me no matter how far I drifted from Him.

Myself and a couple of other youth leaders began taking groups walking in our local Mourne Mountains, but more often than not I found that I was going off on my own. Increasingly I found these times of solitude invaluable. At this time I was, along with my brother, trying to develop our business, provide for my wife and family and still devote time to Christian Youth work. I know this is no more than countless other people have done, but frankly at times I found the pressure almost unbearable; but I did discover a safety valve. I found when I was on my own in the hills, the trials of life had a wonderful habit of sliding into insignificance, or at least a reasonable perspective.

Time and again I found that having left home with the cares of the world on my shoulders, (to the point where on a few occasions I was wondering was life really worth living) I would return feeling calm and re-energized, ready to face the morrow. It wasn't just me who noticed the difference, for I can remember a few occasions when my wife 'tactfully' suggested that perhaps it was time I was going for a walk! On these solitary excursions I knew that I was not alone. I found that my relationship with God, which so often at home was dry and powerless, or which in church remained elusive, on the open hill surrounded by His creation became a natural feeling which - uninvited - nevertheless installed itself in my mind. Time and again I would find that I was walking along thinking of Him, praising Him and praying. What a joy and reassurance it was, and is, to sense this feeling of closeness.

(William Plunkett)

I can remember times when I have felt alone: moments in my life when I feel I can do nothing right and when I am hindered by fears, frustrations, worry and doubts. They are times when I feel distant from God, and in these times I know what it is to feel restless. I remember during one of these times feeling the urge to go outside, just to walk and to forget. But it wasn't a time to forget. It was a time to face up to what I was experiencing. It was time to meet with God. As I stumbled away from civilization, I met with Him. I could see Him, feel Him, and hear Him, more clearly than I had for a long time. I felt His love powerfully there among all the natural wonder that He has created.

Soon after, in church, during the time of worship on a Sunday morning, I experienced a new depth because of the memories I had: memories of being out and looking at what God has made and being in awe of His power. I can sing of His majesty, splendour and glory, because, through what He has made, I have come to understand these aspects of His character more fully. For me, getting out there, leaving the world behind, and focusing on Jesus is one of the most liberating and freeing experiences I have ever felt in my life.

(Jordan Turk)

I was brought up in a Christian home and was involved in a church until my late teens. Somehow at that time, I allowed myself to be distracted by the lies of the world. It felt like I only took my eyes off Jesus for a moment, but in that moment I somehow lost sight of the truth, so much so, that eventually I could not even remember what it was. Almost ten years passed and I became restless. I felt as though I was living a half-life, and nothing I did brought me any kind of peace.

One night I was out in town with some friends. We were at a Halloween party and afterwards on the street, a man, no doubt under the influence of some illegal substance, walked past me muttering. As he passed, he looked me straight in the eye with utter contempt while cursing and swearing under his breath. In that moment I had a strong feeling of the evil that is present in the world around us. All around me, people were spilling out of pubs, and staggering about the streets. Somebody had been sick beside a lamppost. Arguments were taking place between couples. Other people were flirting, hoping for someone to accompany them home for the night. I turned and ran home to my parent's house; I did not want to be alone in my flat that night.

A couple of weeks later I sat in the alcove seat of my attic room, with the skylight window opened as far as it would go. I could see for miles - as far as the distant hills. I thought about the incident a couple of weeks earlier and how I had found it so easy to believe in the presence of evil, but not so easy to believe in the presence of God. As I looked out of the window, the scene in front of me lit up as the sun came out, and great shafts of sunlight illuminated the distant hills. My heart and spirit were lifted as I gazed at the image of beauty before me. Such a contrast between it and the memory of that night in town.

I then had what I can only describe as a revelation. I became aware of God in a way that I never had before. I realized that He is the love in the relationships I have with friends and family. He is in the beauty of a painting, a sculpture, even a building. He is in every colour and scent of the natural world I could see from my window. All good things I could see through my tainted eyes are mere glimmers and reflections of God's glory and hold such promise of what is yet to come. Any time I want to be close to God, I sit there by that window, read His word, and gaze out over His creation. God is a God of no limits.

('Creator', Marie Dorrat)

Throughout my Christian life there have been various key moments where I have met God in new and exciting ways. However, my times spent with God in the hills have been very different to anything else I have experienced and the memories and feelings from those times will be with me for the rest of my life.

On one occasion I remember standing at the foot of the hills and feeling absolute awe for God's creation. I felt I had to keep on climbing and from here on I began to pay closer attention to how God's creation revealed itself to me. By now I was singing out loud giving thanks to God. The terrain became more difficult but it didn't slow me down.

As I rested, taking in the stunning scenery, God's peace came upon me. I reflected on how the landscape had become more impressive the higher I climbed. God was saying to me that his plans for me are far greater than the little things I had envisaged. I needed to trust God and step out in faith. I knew that I had heard this before but in this place I could see it clearly, emphasized through the action of climbing, and I began to believe it like never before. I was excited because although this was a simple word from God it was timely. I was going to be a dad in a couple of months time and I knew that I needed to take responsibility for the spiritual direction of not just myself but for my family.

God made a big impression on my life that day. As I descended the mountain I was excited, not daunted, by the challenges that lay ahead. In my mind, my God was again a mighty creative God who is in control of every aspect of my life.

(Jonathan Barclay)

My first 'wilderness experience' was like coming off a roller coaster ride at Disney World and going straight onto a sailing ship on calm waters. The busyness of my life often feels like a roller coaster.

Even out amongst some incredible scenery my mind was telling me I was still on the roller coaster. My head was spinning; I couldn't really absorb this breath-taking experience. I kind of felt like I didn't belong here! City life, traffic, noise, pollution, telephones ringing, appointments to be kept - that's what I was really used to. Being out here was like a 'cold turkey' experience. I was struggling to take it all in. The waterfall, rolling hills, the mountains, greenery, sheep and the sweet, sweet smell of nature was almost too much for my brain!

I eventually began to slow down and listen. The sound of the countryside is so unusual. I could feel God filling my senses. I started to feel renewed, as strange as that may sound. I began to pay attention to things I hadn't really considered before. Even small flowers - they seemed so colourful!

I remember going for a walk to find a quiet spot to meditate on God's creation. I sat down next to a large rock in order that I could shelter from the wind. As I lay on the grass, I could see a flower nodding in the wind next to me. I found myself just staring at it. It seemed like I was gazing at it for ages. I've never spent more than a few seconds looking at flowers before. It was amazing. I felt excited about it. Me, getting excited about looking at a flower. This was indeed a new experience for me!

Renewed, exhilarated, de-stressed, peaceful, excited, grateful, these are just a few of the adjectives I can use to describe the after affects of my encounter with God's creation.

('My First Wilderness Experience', Adrian Turk)

Have you ever felt stressed out even though your day has been quiet and uneventful? When you take a deep breath and feel the tension in your shoulders but can't quite put your finger on what is causing it. Often hours in an office in a sedentary job can do this to a person, and it was on a day like this that I thought I would spend my lunch break in the car (well, a habit of laziness is difficult to break.) So I drove a couple of miles in no particular direction, idly turning the wheel whatever way felt easiest. And suddenly, upon turning a corner I happened across a very beautiful spot to park, and couldn't possibly have stayed in the car. It was merely minutes away from the dull lifeless building I spent hours in every day, yet I had never known this place existed.

I followed a leaf-covered, muddy path alongside rushing torrents of water creating a noisy backdrop to the serene, secret place I had just been led to. God had known my need that day, and the surprise I felt when I discovered this little corner of the world made me smile from ear to ear. Instantly I was freed from the stress - the weariness I had not even realized was there - and I returned to the workplace like a new person."

('Secret Place In The City', Karen Dorrat)

I love being 3000 feet high; roaming the highest mountain ranges that Scotland has to offer. It is there that I feel most relaxed.

It is not just the awesome natural beauty that so powerfully reflects God. It is the still calmness that comes from standing on a summit and seeing spread all around the variety of scenery that the Creator has commanded into being. I experience a joy, and peace and feel confident in all that God has promised. It is as though each hill gives me another chapter, or another verse, into my Father's heart. As though God opens my eyes more with every step. I understand the power of God more, as the wind buffets against me and whips the breath from my mouth. I know His tenderness as I find some unexpected colour in a tiny flower that clings to a high rocky crag. I stumble upon various forms of wildlife, living quiet lives in remote wild places, all of it looked after by a loving God.

Each moment spent in these places deepens my relationship with God. An intimacy is developed through spending time simply basking in the glory of what He has made. I thank God that what I see in this world is just a fraction of what awaits us in eternity.

God's voice commanded and the seas separated, mountains soared high, crashing up through the land. Stars scattered illuminating the skies at night, dancing behind the moon. The sun rose with an intensity man can never reach. I take pleasure in the knowledge that I am part of this creation plan."

('Outside Looking Up', Ewan Mitchell)

REVELATION

"Come and Listen,
Come to the waters edge,
All you who are thirsty come.
Let me tell you what He has done for me.
Let me tell you what He has done for me,
He has done for you,
He has done for us,
Come and listen"
(David Crowder, 'Come and Listen', 2005)

The single beam of light cuts a swathe through the darkness of a freezing April predawn. As the single-track road twists and turns, climbs and falls, the little 125cc motorbike carries me steadily away from the last orange glow of street-lights and houses. There is little sense of freedom despite the open road stretching out in front for all I feel is the pain in my freezing joints. I wear all the insulated walking kit I have, in the hope that it will keep me warm on this journey, as well as in the wilds. Still the cold is penetrating every layer. I now shiver continually and long

for the car park at the foot of the climb and the start point
for the walk I have planned.

At last the bike sits alone, at the edge of a little gravel-
patch called a car park, and I set off at a jog. I keep the
helmet on my head as I run, desperate to warm my blood
and feel its heat flow through my body. The desire to meet
God had been powerful enough to have me up and out of
the warm bed and heated house, and off into the darkness
at three thirty in the morning. I wanted to meet with God,
and had felt drawn out into the wilder areas of Scotland.
Now nearing six o'clock I was moving, as fast as frozen joints
would allow, away from all things man-made.

It was more than streetlights and houses and a warm
bed that I was leaving behind. Lindsay and I had been
married for a year and were more in love than ever. She was,
still is, and always will be, my wife, companion, best friend
and much more. We had a great home together and she was
sailing through a postgraduate in fine art with flying colors
- quite literally! I had a secure job as a tree surgeon - well
- as secure as a job climbing sick and dying trees can be! We
were part of a vibrant and expanding church. A church of
people who were personally and collectively drawing closer
to the heart of God. I had plenty of time for sports and was
enjoying finishing in some decent positions in the Scottish
Cycle Racing and Mountain Bike scenes. I even had time to
dabble in a bit of hill running and rock climbing as well! On
top of all the sports, I was learning to play bass guitar and
was getting involved in the worship team.

On the surface all looked well, and most of the time
it was. Every now and then though, when I paused from
all the action and thought about it, there was a niggling
sense or feeling that I needed to realign my life to that
which God had planned. I was following God and life was
good. However, somehow I knew there was more. I felt an
underlying emptiness and needed some time away from all
the buzz and whir of life to really look at where God was
leading me. And so it was with this backdrop that I found
myself jogging through the darkness in the middle of some
of Scotland's wildest landscape, wearing all of my walking

gear - and a motorbike helmet!

For my wild walk, I hadn't planned to follow any paths, but it did feel strange to simply turn off the road at a random point and start stumbling through the heather. With the ascent came the sought after heat. It was time to stash the helmet, to be picked up again later for the return torturous motorbike journey! Removing the helmet brought an immediate sense of connection with the landscape around me. While I had worn the helmet it felt like I was in a little self-contained world, like being inside, and looking out from, a goldfish bowl I guess. Now, all around, the world seemed real, alive, and even in the half-light of dawn, intensely packed with beauty. With the helmet on, I had breathed air through a fine mesh; heard sound muffled through the protective layers, and watched a distorted world through the cheap plastic visor. With the helmet off, here on the edge of the wilderness, I now stood ready for a day that would shape the course of my life to come.

I climbed directly up the slope, knowing that high above me lay a vast wild plateau that is renowned for its semi-arctic conditions and associated plant and animal-life. It is an area rarely visited even by ardent hill-walkers. By the time I reached its edge, light had filled the sky and day had arrived. Before me stretched a vast expanse of heather, grass, stone, snow-fields and rolling summits. The snow had a stunning translucent glow, as though it was lit from deep below its frozen crust. I felt a familiar sense of detachment from everyday life. It was as though I could look back on my life and assess it from a distance. It was a good life, and yet here I was with this niggling conviction that I was missing something. In my life, I was on a good path, yet I knew that God had a perfect path laid out for me. I wanted to find it. I wanted my life to be realigned. I did not want to settle for mediocrity when God's way is perfect. I wanted to follow His path for my life and no other.

I walked and walked and with each step came a sense of lightness and relief. I walked and prayed and thought and questioned. I walked and praised and prayed and wondered. All I could see was wild creation in every direction. My life seemed so far away, over the edge of the plateau and down the single-track road, through villages and towns. I could imagine myself, still in bed, waking up beside Lindsay with a smile on my face. But I wasn't. I was in a land of snow and wildness. What was I doing? Why was I here? Where on earth was I going?

I asked these questions and many more as I walked and prayed and sat on that high plateau. And for most, as I asked, I realized I already knew the answer. Why did I feel pointlessness at times? Because I had deviated from what God had planned. Simple. Why did I feel frustration? Because on the path I would stride easily along, but off it I would trip and stumble and blame everything around me, rather than acknowledge that I had left the track. Question after question, answer after answer. I knew that I was saved and that life eternal stretched out before me, but I was also more convinced than ever that God's love transcended all boundaries. I knew that I had a life here and now that could be lived to its fullest, in close relationship with God, and in the excitement and joy that comes through following His way alone.

What was stopping me? What was holding me back from stepping onto that path that God wanted me to be on? I was walking again now. The sun was beating down from blue skies above. I wandered along in a stupor, hardly remembering getting up or making the decision to do so. Here sandwiched between the earth and heavens I wandered, with my life exposed, open, and ready to be changed. With each step words that described barriers that were stopping me getting back on track revolved in my head - pride, fear, stubbornness, self-reliance, confusion, haste, independence and many more. I had been too proud to admit that I was off track. I had an illogical fear of getting back on. I was confused because I had thought that all the sporting pursuits that I had hastily pursued would bring the purpose and meaning I sought, but they hadn't. I wanted everything to happen in my timing, and I wanted to do it myself. With each step, and each recognition and acknowledgement of a barrier, I let go of some of my selfishness. And for every step there was a tear. Letting go hurt a lot! In the end I realized that it came down to this: "God, Your ways, not my ways." At the time I wasn't even sure if that was from scripture, but that was what filled my mind as I knelt in the snow with tears on my cheeks and my face turned toward the blue skies above. I knew that I had been going my own way far too long. I knew that my hope had been misplaced. Now it was over to God. With that decision made, the process of change could begin. Every little bit of life that I had been holding back for myself was now handed over. I knew then that no matter what it took I would follow God's way.

I was up again, and walking, my steps crunching over glowing snow. I knew some things for certain. I knew I was going to go back and change some things in my life. I felt a conviction that it was time to change my career. Some of my sporting pursuits were going to end. My bass guitar could go to the base of a storage box. All the things I had misplaced hope of finding significance in, I wanted to get rid of or realign. My life was going to change and this change would bring challenges but I felt a certainty that I was making the right decisions. It felt great to have a sense of complete realignment of my life. The hazy muddle of uncertainty that had filled my mind had gone. What an amazing day. And then an amazing sequence of events occurred.

Walking across another snowfield I came across a huge hole, in the middle of which flowed a clear stream of water. The sun beat down and all around was purest blue and white. I drank water from a burn so cold that it felt as though it burned my throat. I scooped more into my cup and lay back against my rucksack on the snow. The trickling water was the only sound. A lizard scuttled out from the edge of the stream and across the snow. It paused to look at me then scuttled off over the edge of the snowfield and into the heather. I had no idea that lizards inhabited the area, and was surprised to see a cold-blooded creature scurrying about on the snow. I was alone but for this little reptilian life, and the great creator God. As quickly and unexpectedly as the little lizard had scuttled into view, I felt the presence of God more powerfully than I ever had. I felt I should stand, or kneel, but so powerful was the unexpected sensation that I just lay there stunned, holding my breath. A shiver pulsed through my body. Not because of the snow below but because of God, because of the Holy Spirit. It was the sort of shiver that causes every hair on the body to stand on end. Then I was on my knees. I felt like I should speak, but no words seemed adequate for responding to or for praising such an awesome God. I spoke anyway, words that would make no sense to the human ear. I just had to make some sound of praise. I thought the day had been great before, when my questions were being answered and my negative feelings lifting as I brought everything before God and repented. Now it surpassed all expectations.

I don't know how long I sat there with more tears rolling down my cheeks, and a smile spread across my face. I soon noticed the cold of the snow on my knees and I sat back again against the rucksack. I had felt the presence of the God of the universe. Over the rim of the snow ran two hares, still half dressed in their white winter fur, and half in summer brown, contrasting sharply against the snow. They hopped and jumped and chased each other, seemingly oblivious to me watching. I had already seen many hares that day, but they had darted away from me with incredible speed. These two hopped and jumped with twisting moves that would have been the envy of any gymnast. A shrill song came from a bird high above, adding melody to the bass notes of the burn. Two Ptarmigan, birds that loves these high wild places, suddenly flew into the scene, swooping and diving, and flying close to and around each other. I sat and continued to praise God. It was as though all of His wild creation responded to Him, wanting to be where His presence had been most obvious.

Amidst this arena of freedom I sat stunned. Everywhere I looked, my eyes were met with graceful movement and purity. All around me was simplicity. All creation seemed to praise, and so did I. It was in that context of praise and awe that I knew in an instant that part of the course God had laid out before me would involve leading others out into wild places such as this, where I now sat. I knew that I would not be a mountain guide, or an expedition leader in the common sense, but that I would lead people out specifically for the purpose of meeting God amidst His wild creation. It seemed outrageous, even absurd, that I had not recognized this calling sooner. But my mind had been filled with barriers and these barriers needed to be dealt with so that I could move on. In a moment of intense intimacy, I experienced His divine love in my life, and I sat there reveling in His attention to detail in all creation, and the details of my life.

The journey home was a blur. And so was the year or two following the wild experience. It was a time requiring discernment, and of seeking the wisdom of trusted friends and respected church leaders, and of leaning on God, and following His guidance rather than logic of my own. Things seemed to happen so fast, and within a relatively short time I was working with people, as opposed to trees and I was soon a qualified mountain leader. In my job, and also in my spare time, opportunities opened up that entailed leading people out into wild creation. I was on the path God had laid before me, and any door I came against seemed to be the automatic sort, for they opened without me even having to push. All I had to do was stay close to God and follow His lead. That was now the easy part, for He had become the hub of my life, around which everything else revolved.

Walking closely to God is exciting and life unfolds as a great adventure. I can look back at my past, and God has given me a glimpse of the ending, but the bit in between is fascinating and exciting. I knew from that day that it was for a specific spiritual purpose that I wanted to lead people into the wilds. As God kept revealing more of the path to me, the idea of 'Spiritual Expeditions' formed. From tree surgeon to leader of Spiritual Expeditions in just a few short years! I do not write any of this to boast, except in the power of God. For without Him at the hub of my life I would still be chasing significance in various sports, hoping, and failing, to find it there. I would have continued to be stuck in my rut of tree surgery, doing a job that was not my calling, because I did not know what else to do. Without God at the core, I would have missed out on the greatest adventure, and settled for mediocrity.

On my Mountain Leadership training course, I found myself in an area not far from the wild plateau where my life had changed so dramatically that day. From a summit I gazed across and let my eyes sweep over the vast area on which I had walked and stumbled and knelt and cried a couple of years earlier. I felt as though I was looking toward holy ground. I know God is everywhere, and that He was as much with me on the Mountain Leader Course as anywhere else, but as I stood there, I gazed at the area with memories of the most powerful and intimate time with the great Creator of all.

A year or two after the Mountain Leader Course, Lindsay and I ascended another couple of hills to the east of the plateau. We had camped in the beautiful valley just below and had carried our little eight month old daughter up toward the summit of her first Munro, after her first night of wild camping. She loved it! Once again I gazed out across the wild plateau, and standing there beside Lindsay, with Adara on my back, I was more convinced than ever that I am on the path that God wants me to be.

Throughout this period of rapid change, and often times of living in faith (certainly on the financial side of things), Lindsay was incredible. She never doubted or questioned that this new path was from God. The role for Lindsay was and still is much more than that of a supportive wife. During this time of rapid change for me, God was simultaneously developing in her a vision and dream that positively impacts many people. Lindsay dreams of seeing creativity as an integral part of worship, and of Christian life as a whole, and is giving herself to pursuing that vision. But that is another story! If we each follow the unique path God has laid out before us then there is no limit to what we can achieve in our short time here on earth. We all need time away from the distractions of a busy world to simply listen to what our Father is saying and to seek the path He has for us.

That special day a few years ago, as I walked over the physical landscape of wild creation, I simultaneously set out over the much unexplored and unmapped spiritual landscape. It was as though the spiritual landscape and the physical landscape connected and collided in an incredibly tangible way. As a result I will shout from the highest hilltops and the deepest valley floors. I will shout it from loch-shores, and forests, from fields and from mountains. I will shout it from wherever I am, that we all need to do what Christ did and get to a place where we can spend uninterrupted time alone with our Father. We need to meet intimately with our Father who longs to fill our lives with meaning and purpose and joy. We need to stop, be quiet, and listen. We need to hear His call.

I have told you my story. Now I urge you to go and listen. Go now to a place of beauty and peace and stillness. Listen. Hear. What is He saying to you?

Bibliography

Here are just a few recommended books if you wish to take your exploration of this subject further:

Bratton, Susan Power, *Christianity, Wilderness and Wildlife: The Original Desert Solitaire*, Associated University Presses 1993

Brown, Hamish, *Hamish's Mountain Walk: The First Traverse of all the Scottish Munros in One Journey*, London Victor Gollancz Ltd., 1978

Cartwright Austin, Richard, *Baptized into Wilderness: A Christian Perspective on John Muir*, John Knox Press, 1987.

Eldredge, John, *Waking the Dead: The Glory of a Heart Fully Alive*, Thomas Nelson Publishers, 2003

Havner, Vance, *In Tune with Heaven*, Baker Book House Company 1990

Langmuir, Eric, *Mountaincraft and Leadership: A Handbook for Mountaineers and Hillwalking Leaders in the British Isles*, The Scottish Sports Council and the MLTB, 1995

Macfarlane, Robert, *Mountains of the Mind: A History of Fascination*, Granta Books, 2003

McNeish, Cameron, *The Wilderness World of Cameron McNeish: Essays From Beyond the Black Stump*, The In Pinn, 1988.

Muir, John, *The Wilderness Journeys: Story of My Boyhood and Youth 1913, A Thousand Mile Walk to the Gulf 1916, My First Summer in the Sierra 1911, Travels in Alaska 1915, Stickeen 1909*, Published in a single volume by Canongate Classics, 1996

Muir, John, *The Mountains of California*, The American Museum of Natural History, 1961

Murray, W.H. *Mountaineering in Scotland and Undiscovered Scotland: The Author's two Scottish Mountaineering Classics Combined in One Volume*, Diadem Books, 1979

Scottish Literary Tour Company Ltd. (ed), *Land Lines: An Illustrated Journey through the Landscape and Literature of Scotland*, Polygon at Edinburgh, 2001

Smythe, F. S., *The Spirit of the Hills*, Hodder and Stoughton, 1937

About the Author

Born in Ireland, Jon spent his school years and early teens there, surrounded by fields, forests and wild countryside. He left Ireland to study forestry in the Highlands of Scotland, and there spent even more time cycling, running and walking over mountains, through woodlands and in other wild places.

Jon now lives in Scotland with his wife, Lindsay and daughter Adara and has a second child on the way. Jon is qualified in mountain leadership through the Scottish Mountain Leader Training Board, and has an Open University degree in social policy.

Jon works with people with learning disabilities, leading them out into the wild lands of Scotland. He is also the founder of 'Spiritual Expeditions.' These expeditions involve leading people away from towns and cities and out into wild creation with the specific purpose of meeting with God.

www.spiritualexpeditions.com